The Flight to Freedom

By: Trina Frierson

PUBLISHING HOUSE, LLC.

The Flight to Freedom:

By: Katrinia Frierson

Published by:

VJ PUBLISHINGHOUSE, LLC.

20451 NW 2nd Avenue Suite112 Miami Gardens, Fl. 33169

Phone:786-535-9598

www.vjpublishinghouse.com

vjpublishinghouse@gmail.com

ISBN#: 978-1-939236-18-0 (Hardcover)

PRINTED IN THE UNITED STATES OF AMERICA.

THIS BOOK IS PRINTED ON ACID-FREE PAPER.

"Don't focus on the past.

Instead,

Embrace future possibilities."

Katrina "Trina" Frierson

MENDING HEARTS FOUNDER, PRESIDENT & CEO

IN LOVING MEMORY OF

'MAMA'

~Dedication~

I want to take this time to thank the woman of my dreams.

Verta Mae Frierson

Mama, I could not have thought of any other woman who could have taken your challenge with the six of us and made it all worthwhile. I know that many children regret all the things they think they should have had, but I'm grateful for all that was given, which was your dedication and unwavering love that you gave to your children. I'm a better person because you and my kids that you worried about turned out to be more than I could have imagined. I apologize for the life you witnessed in your later days; I know you can now see the true fruits of your labor. I owe it all to you.

Because of you, I had the courage to change and make the sacrifice to have a better life.

~Acknowledgments~

No matter what accomplishments
you make, somebody helped you.
Althea Gibson

Writing a book is something I could have never imagined and was definitely not on my bucket list. I am truly thankful for my mom, who is the reason I survived a life that was not in her forecast. You never gave up on me in my worst times of life struggles. Thank you for being a praying Mama!

To my brother and sisters, I love you despite our flaws and differences. You showed me how to love and continue to be my family.

My children, thank you for allowing me to re-enter your life after the abandonment and neglect that I caused due to my addiction. I'm honored to be a part of your circle, and I do not take it for granted. I understand that it's a privilege to be considered your mother!

Vernon Winfrey, thank you for being a community activist and engaging communities in selflessness. You gave me my first job at the age of 12 and helped me understand that community is the extended family that continues to evolve when things start to crumble.

Ali Marlow, thank you for having the courage to challenge me to change my attitude, behavior, and actions. It's because of you that I have over two decades of recovery. You will never be forgotten, and I know my Mama is forever grateful that you stepped in to help save my kids from losing their mother to a life of destruction.

Jeff Blum, thanks for taking the justice system into your own hands ~~and~~ creating a space for women who need long-term treatment. It works, and I thank you so much.

Charlotte Grant, thank you for coming into my life after our addictive episodes at Dickerson Rd and East Nashville. We were meant to be at that time to encourage one another. Your motivation behind every idea I came to you is my willingness to continue today. The energy you provided while we were taking on the world was tremendous to the growth of Mending Hearts and our family. Thank you for being you!

Joyce Edwards, the moment I mentioned the idea of helping others to you, you continued to pour into me in a way that no one had ever done besides my Mama. Thank you for writing the first check to open the bank account for Mending Hearts and for the countless acts of kindness that you've done to make our mission what it is today.

Shari Tisch, you made volunteering a state-of-the-art activity, being one of the most significant members ever. You came in and rolled up your sleeve to make sure the women at Mending Hearts' needs were met. Thank you.

Janet Warfield, I am writing this book today because of you! You have shown me what true loyalty is and encouraged me year after year to continue to write, and now that we are here, I must thank you wholeheartedly for all you have done to encourage me. It would take me writing another book to tell all the stories that came along the way, but I'm genuinely grateful to you and the entire **Warfield family** for extending your unconditional love to me. Thank you, **buddy**!!!

To the **TDMHSAS (Tennessee Department Mental Health Substance Abuse Services)**, thank you for allowing an ex-offender to assist in advocating and providing services to others of similar circumstances. It's because of your dedication through education and funding that we have footprints in the city of Nashville Tn to help those in need.

Dr. Linda Hazel, thank you for providing individual and family therapy to my entire family. We continue to role play some of the techniques for communication when we are face with barriers amongst siblings.

To **all my anonymous donors and volunteers** who have entered my life, your thoughts and presence have gifted me, whether from knowledge, monetary, or bricks and mortar; this has been an amazing journey on "**The Flight to Freedom**."

TABLE OF CONTENTS

~About the Author~

Whenever there is a gathering or celebration event at the Mending Hearts office (which occurs frequently; they love to celebrate!), you will hear chants of "Trina, Trina..." combined with cheers and loud applause from the clients and staff in attendance. The ladies love her, the staff loves her, and the community in which Trina tirelessly serves loves her. The Mending Heart family celebrates Trina in her successful, miraculous recovery and her tireless effort in the recovery and aid of others.

One special note about Trina is that she is relatable. She's real. She can not only dialogue with the leaders and government officials in the city of Nashville, speak on stage in front of massive audiences and be a leader in policy and committee meetings on boards of organizations around the city, but she helps the maintenance worker at her office, she spends time with the ladies at Mending Hearts and listens to their stories. And she is happy to share her days of active addiction and what it was like in her recovery. She provides a source of hope and encouragement in a down-to-earth, relatable, and effective way. Mending Hearts has become one of the model agencies in the state of Tennessee, the most prominent female-only facility in the state, and it all began with the care and help she offered to one lady by sharing what resources she had and letting her sleep on her couch in 2002.

"When the ladies come in from various walks of life – from under a bridge, jail, off the street, or from a broken home, I see their brokenness and despair. But beyond the physical and spiritual death that they carry in their countenance, I see light in them. There is still hope despite their depleted, deteriorated, distorted appearance. Hope is there, but most of all, what I see is – for the sake of God, there goes I. I see me in them," quotes Trina. Trina's approach is one that helped her in her recovery – the first step is in practicing Maslow's hierarchy of needs in providing shelter, clothing, and food, but also recognizing that it goes beyond the basic core needs, being able to recognize that behind the behavior that created the drug dependency are mental health issues that cause deterioration masked by the drugs. "My biggest question is, how do we best help them? How do we help them move forward?" Trina concludes. "Mending Hearts helps the women to draw out a game plan for recovery, knowing they have support. Addicts respond better with others who have similarities in their recovery journey."

~Preface~

Within you is the ability to rise above any circumstance that you may be facing while transforming into the most proficient, purposeful person you can be.

Rise from within before you begin.

Difficult roads may lead to better designation...

Trina Frierson

~Chapter One~

'The Little Girl from North 5th Street'

It's not the load that breaks you down.

It's the way you carry it.

Lena Horne

Childhood experiences form the basis of who you are until you become a whole individual. The brain's formation and maturation happen until you reach the age of 25. However, most of that growth happens during your life's first five to ten years. How you look at the world, think when bad things happen, and deal with the good have their foundation in your childhood. So, it makes sense for any good story based on anyone's life, to begin with childhood rather than somewhere in the middle. The human memory does not function like a journal; it does not sequentially take note of what happened in the day like a computer log. It tends to be more random. We remember the strangest things from our childhood. Some memories seemed inconsequential and mundane when they were lived, yet they became so special later on.

An example of this from my own life is that I might not exactly remember what I had for dinner last night, but I do remember how it felt to hold my mother's hand on a crisp spring morning. We walked to kindergarten, I was five, and the wind was nice. I remember how it felt on my face as we walked towards the school. I do not recall the times after school when I went home, but the mornings are what I do remember—perhaps because it was just my mother and me. She was always chipper in the morning and would point out the clouds in the sky as we walked. My mother would always leave me at school on a positive note, ensuring we parted on happy terms. I never let my mood be anything other than happy when the school day began.

It was safer back then, walking on the streets. Much calmer. Much more peaceful. It might seem like an alien concept nowadays, but I do not recall us having to lock our doors when we slept at night.

Sometimes, we would even doze off watching TV on the porch, never a worry for our safety from shadowy figures in the night. ACs were not as common back then as they are today; in fact, all I remember was the box fans, and we had one in each room to cool the house in the hot Tennessee summers. We sometimes came onto the porch and slept in the cool night air. We could play outside much later; our parents did not panic if the sun was down, and the kids were late for supper as long as we were in sight of the house. My mom was more worried about us getting to bed on time than about anything untoward that might have occurred to any of us.

I lived in Nashville, TN; we had a house on the corner of North 5th and Bayard. To date, it is at the corner of North 5th and Vernon Winfrey Blvd. But I remember spending many nights playing at my friend's house that my mother could view from our home. For some reason, I could never get her to agree to any sleepovers beforehand. Our house was like a community house, with our friends staying over and spending their time with us. And it was not just for holidays; they would come on the weekdays, and we would have dinner together as the parents commiserated and hung out with each other.

We were in a well-knitted neighborhood, and our family was relatively close, too. Our neighborhood was poor; however, we were rich in the love we shared with everyone in our community. There were six of us, the siblings, and my mother did all that she could for us. There was always much work around the house; she did it with a smile, never complaining. She worked two jobs and came home to make dinner for her babies. It did not matter how old we were; we were always her babies. And we still are.

We were forced to move from Hines Street to a low-income housing project in east Nashville. It was known as Seattle Court.

We were only in the Settle Court Projects for a little while; things were less safe there than in our previous home. My mother had misgivings about the place, but it was not until our bikes were stolen that she decided it was time to move.

Hines Street held many memories—good, bad, and bittersweet. Childhood memories are like rare gems hidden in the depths of our minds, waiting to be dug. They shimmer with the hues of innocence and laughter, carrying us on a magical journey to a time when the world was more straightforward and wonderfully danced in every corner.

These memories can transport us back to days when the sun seemed brighter, and the days stretched endlessly. It's like flipping through the pages of a cherished storybook, each memory a chapter filled with petrichor (that beautiful smell after the rain), the taste of sugary treats, and the echo of carefree laughter-.

The sound of a childhood song, the touch of a worn-out toy, or the taste of a favorite meal – they all weave a tapestry of emotions that pull at our heartstrings. It's a journey that tugs at our souls, reminding us of the simple joys that once brought unfiltered happiness.

As we navigate the complexities of adulthood, there's comfort in reliving those days when worries were as distant as the stars. They become a sanctuary where we can escape, if only for a moment, to a place where scraped knees were badges of courage and imagination knew no bounds.

The beauty of it lies not just in the memories themselves but in the emotions they evoke. It's the warmth of a mother's embrace, the excitement of a first adventure, and the camaraderie of childhood friendships — all frozen in time, waiting to rekindle the fire of our spirits.

It's a celebration of the laughter, the tears, and the love that painted our childhood canvas. And in that celebration, I am reminded of easter egg hunts. They were more than just a childhood tradition. They were the threads that wove the colorful tapestry of my upbringing, memories that still shimmer in the corners of my mind. Mr. Zelda's house, an unassuming house three doors down from ours, was the epicenter of these joyous quests. Every-year, it seemed, we gathered in eager anticipation, knowing that even if the elusive golden egg remained out of reach, a prize awaited us, nonetheless. The lessons in kindness and inclusion were hidden amidst the hunt for brightly painted treasures.

But beyond the excitement of the hunt, something about shoes captivated me as a child. While one of the most popular shoes was the Chuck Taylors, they were different from my liking, although I was spared a few pairs. It was The Pro-Keds tennis shoes; oh, how they were my cherished companions! Adorned in various colors, they mirrored my youthful spirit – vibrant and unapologetically expressive. In a world untouched by the opulence of Gucci or the allure of Prada, my family cherished the finest of simplicity.

Despite financial constraints, my mother's artistry in dressing us was unparalleled. Some clothes were bought, while others were carefully chosen from yard sales and Goodwill, transformed into ensembles that defied their humble origins.

Those early years in East Nashville were a tapestry of curiosities, wild onions, and Polk salad gathered from vacant yards. My mother, a beacon of wisdom, would demonstrate that nature's bounty lay hidden in plain sight, waiting for us to awaken to its gifts. And then there was the building on the corner of Rosa Parks and Eighth Avenue North – a peculiar gathering place. People would line up, jugs in hand, for the strange sulfur water that flowed from its side. The pungent odor of rotten eggs accompanied the conviction that this water held transformative powers. Despite the skepticism, my mother's unwavering belief mirrored the tenacity of generations past – a tribute to the resilience borne from adversity.

While sulfur water held its appeal, my heart longed for the simpler joys of Kool-Aid. The clink of ice cubes and companions' laughter made it a symphony of summer afternoons. Paired with a tuna fish sandwich or a fried bologna creation, it was a sensory delight that transcended the mundane. Yet I can never forget when we struggled to make a sandwich, and the only ingredients the sandwich was made of were ketchup or sugar. We were happy and satisfied in the hard times if we had a good old egg sandwich. There were a few days, not many days were spent like this, but we did experience them, and as of today, I have no regrets. These moments etched in time were part of the collective consciousness of a community that understood the value of shared experiences.

"Project Kool-Aid" became a testament to the pursuit of perfection – the right balance of sweetness that mirrored life's delicate equilibrium. "Project Kool-Aid" symbolized resilience, the ability to withstand challenges with unwavering strength. These utterances were not mockery but badges of honor.

I remember when my father worked on a car in the front

yard. I was having a tussle with my brother Gerald. My mother was very calm-spirited; she had to be with six kids. However, there were times when she had to raise her voice; this was one of those times. You see, Gerald was bigger than I was. When our fight turned physical, he could physically haul me around, given that no parent was in the immediate vicinity. My arm hit the woodburning furnace we used to heat the house during this struggle. It was a terrible burn. The average kid might expect a beating, but my brother got a good tongue-lashing from my mother. The fact that she was usually so cool made it compelling; Gerald thought twice about any tussle afterward.

In any case, I was not rushed to the hospital. We treated most things the good old way during those times at home. If worst came to worst and you needed medicine, you just went to the neighborhood drug store. Apart from that, we had home cures and remedies. My mother kept some bacon fat and salve that she would use for bruises and injuries to prevent infection, along with some gauze when required. And that was that. My mother even kept an Aloe Vera plant; she used its gel to treat burns. Bootleg healthcare was not the only indicator that we were poor; when we did not have hot water, my mama would heat pans on the stove for the kids to bathe with. Because there were so many of us, there were many trips from the kitchen to the bathroom before we were presentable. When it got cold, she would bundle us up in layers and layers of clothing, so we did not get sick. She would try and develop ways to feed us that were cheap but healthy. Her soup was famous in the neighborhood. She used packs of ramen and some chicken and fixings; we loved how good it was. Other times, she just put together rice, butter, and sugar to make sweet treats for us. My mama was the best cook in the world. She could make pancakes and fried chicken better than any restaurant ever could from scratch.

My mother had a lot to do, and she was always resourceful in everything she did. She had to be, to manage all of what she did.

I was quite a curious child. My mother was never too harsh towards us, and so my curiosity about the world was left to grow relatively unrestricted. I followed my mother around and tried to emulate her as a kid. I remember trying to cook; I could turn the stove on at age four, and by five, I remember cooking bacon for myself. There were times when I got into trouble as well. One time, I came across a firecracker. I was trying to figure out what it was. My mother used to smoke, and I thought that it was something you smoked. With my curiosity getting the best of me, I lit the other side of the firecracker as if it were a cigarette and then put it in my mouth.

As I tried to breathe in, the firecracker went off in sparks, and my mouth became collateral damage. My mouth was severely hurt. There were blisters inside my mouth and my throat. I had trouble eating during that time.

Despite being so busy, my mother always found time for us. Whether over dinner, in the kitchen, or while distributing some homemade snacks, she made sure to get the family together and spend time with and talk to us. She told me she did not want us to be like her, poor and living hand to mouth, and wanted us to get educated. Her teaching and spirit made me want to do good in life, whereas many of my peers fell off soon into their schooling. She only had an eighth-grade education and had to work two jobs to support us.

My mother was also very skilled at social engineering; to handle six kids, you had to be. I recall one time I was on bad terms with my brother, and we were not talking. She would get us to dinner and then put us into situations where the two of us would have to interact. She would tell my brother to pass the salt to me or for me to pass the potatoes to him. It was annoying at the time, but it was how she helped us resolve our sibling feuds.

On top of her jobs, preparing food and taking care of us, she also kept us on good terms with each other, putting out fires before they began. My mother was indeed a remarkable woman. She was my role model, and I was always immensely proud of her. Despite being close to poor, I had a happy childhood, and I have my mother to thank for that. I know she was afraid we would end up like her, but the heart-rending truth is that I would have been immensely grateful to have half my mother's strength.

~Chapter 2~

'The Lady on the Corner'

I was never sure of much as a kid. But the one thing I knew for
sure was that Verta Mae Frierson, my **Mama**, was a
'Phenomenal Woman.'

I always associated my mother with the color white.
Perhaps it was due to the uniform and shoes she was
always in, ready to hustle and make a living. My Mama
was a five-foot-four, dark-skinned woman with an average
build. One of my favorite memories of her is braiding her
silky grey locks, which reminded me of storm clouds when
I came of age. I believed her hair was breath-taking, but
she wasn't fond of it. Mama was like that. She never saw
herself for how beautiful she was.

As much as I loved Mama's hair, I usually saw it covered
by wigs. She was very fond of them. It made me think of
how I would see all these women covering their hair with
wigs one day and then showing off their natural hair the
next. It was a powerful realization, which dawns on me
daily: the freedom one gets when one starts being

themselves. And that's just who my Mama was: unapologetically, little old Verta Mae Frierson!

Mama's focus never wavered. Her path was straightforward: making a living for herself and her babies.

She strutted about in her white uniform and work shoes with her head held high. Most of my friends mistook her for a nurse because of her uniform, and I would always correct them. Mama was not a nurse. She was a supervisor for the hospital's laundry department. Whenever I talked about Mama's occupation, my eyes lit up. Every inch of my face would reflect passion and pride. I would excitedly tell my friends about her duties, like ensuring the hospital had clean linens, towels, and scrubs. I was genuinely proud of my mom because she taught me how to be proud of where I was, no matter what I had. Mama never showed any pride, especially in herself. She was the humblest woman I had ever known. She remained modest about her achievements, like when she received the title of employee of the month and got promotions or raises.

The word that comes to mind when I think about Miss
Verta Mae Frierson is resilient.

This woman would take the bus to work most mornings.
Sometimes, she would catch a ride with one of the
neighbors on our block, but if they shifted departments,
she would be back on that bus without missing a beat. This
remained her daily routine until my eldest son, Hershel,
was old enough to drive, and he ensured she got to work
on time. Even then, there were times when she had no
other option but to take the hectic bus ride; Hershel tried
his best for that not to happen. As my other brothers grew
up, they joined in and helped Mom with the commute, but
it was a different routine for them.

Another thing about Mama was that she demanded
respect. It wasn't out of intimidation or fear. Instead,
people wanted to give her their consideration because of
who she was as a person. I recall one particular incident
when I was in middle school. I broke my finger while
playing basketball, so she had to take me along with her to
work. I cherished that time with her immensely. I was so
obsessed with going with her to work that if I had a

stomachache, I thought it was an excuse to go to the doctor at Ma's hospital, Nashville Metro General Hospital on Hermitage Ave. Mama didn't have the luxury or the money to take time off work if we got sick, so she opted to take us along and hide us in her office.

Her supervisor knew we were there, but we couldn't be on the floor and had to keep our distance from the hospital's equipment. Mama had a way of making me feel like the most special girl in the world. She was well respected by everyone around us, the neighbors, and the kitchen cooks at the hospital. The kitchen staff frequently sent leftovers to our house, assuming we needed a cooked meal when they saw my mother's hectic routine of raising six children. The cooks ensured she had a ride home so she wouldn't have to carry the food on the bus.

Even when Mama cooked leftovers from others, she had a way of making them her own. She added something special to every meal to show us that she put in her love. We couldn't tell if the food was leftovers because it was mouth-watering, and we would gobble it up instantly. As a child, I believed I was her special baby. I thought I was the first to get a bite out of anything she made. Mama had a way with things like that. She made everyone who met her feel special. I got a rude awakening one day when I was bragging about tasting her biscuits, and my brother told me he already had one. It was like someone burst my bubble. I finally thought that maybe I was not the only special one. It wasn't until years later that I found that Mama had her unique way with each of her kids. But as a child, I always wanted to be that one special baby. The thing that proved me wrong was when we were at the dining table, and the conversation started with her telling us how special we were and how we held great importance in her life.

I still have the image of her bright, beaming smile etched into my brain. Her beautiful face lit up when she expressed her love. You could see it in her eyes and how she cooked compassionately and cared for everyone around her. We didn't need her to say it. Her smile spoke volumes about how much she cared. She never aimed to be anything other than a good person by providing for her family and any helpless child in the community who came to our house.   She made it a point to say, *"You all be good to each other,"*

Or *"You all look out for each other. You all are all you got!"*

I carved her words into my memory and tried to live by them. That was probably why my siblings and I always checked in on each other, whether at home or out with friends. I remember one particular early morning when I observed Mama. I either slept in the room on a twin bed or in the bed with Mama. This continued for years until I was about fifteen or sixteen. She would get up early and prepare breakfast for my siblings and friends, who met at our house for school. We lived in the biggest house on the block, but it wasn't the fanciest. I remember holes in the floor and the front porch leaning. It was a five-bedroom and one-bath home, and we made the most of it.

She made sure there were flowers wrapped around the porch, intertwining in a beautiful mix of vibrant colors. Mama had a green thumb. She could bring a dying plant back to life as if it were the easiest task in the world.

Mama's usual routine started with her cooking breakfast, leaving lunch money divided amongst the six of us, and heading to work. This continued until I graduated. We all got the same amount until my older siblings, Brenda, the eldest of the six, started attending a different school. After that, there was Hershel, Freddie, Kenny, and Gerald, and somehow, I became the youngest of the six. After Mama left for work, my sister and some of my brothers went into her bedroom, next to the kitchen, to smoke weed, and at the age of fourteen, I sat around and watched. This is when they would talk, plan their day, and dream of what they would achieve. At least one of them continually asked if I had a basketball game; if I did, they wished me luck.

I missed Mama whenever she left. She remained my rock throughout my life, and when my siblings talked about their dreams, I would only hope that I somehow turned out like the most incredible woman I had ever known, Verta Mae Frierson.

It didn't matter to me what others thought of my mother. All I saw was the most dedicated woman alive. I watched as she left the house daily to work in her white uniform with the shoes to match. A piece of gauze was attached with glue to cover the hole on her shoe around the pinky-toe area. She did that to stop herself from buying new ones for herself. Her only concern was ensuring her kids didn't walk around with holes in their shoes. We never experienced that because of her.

Mama was the supervisor, so she bought many of our clothes from either Goodwill or the neighborhood yard sales, yet she would take them to her job to wash and press so that we could have fresh clothes. That made us feel like we had new stuff all the time. She would bag our clothes up and wash and press them at work to keep her mommy duties up to par as well since she worked two jobs as a single parent.

With determination, Mama broke the chains of generational struggle, fashioning a staircase for us to ascend from the depths of want to the heights of possibility.

Our lives transitioned from scarcity to middle-class comforts. The lessons learned were invaluable—

resourcefulness, empathy, and the power of a single dream. My mother's love nurtured us so profoundly that we never missed out on anything.

She was more than just a parent; she was a guiding light, a beacon of hope that illuminated our path even in the darkest times. As we navigated the complexities of growing up in East Nashville, her love transformed every challenge into an opportunity, every setback into a steppingstone toward a brighter future.

My mother was like a rock in the shifting sands of uncertainty. She never allowed us to feel the weight of our financial limitations. Instead, she wove a world of magic around us, where yard sale finds were turned into treasures, and Goodwill clothing became expressions of individuality. Her hands, skilled in creation, added delicate touches to each piece, turning them into symbols of our uniqueness. She taught us that it's not about what you have but how you present it to the world.

With her optimism, my mother turned nature into a beautiful classroom. Those early years, spent collecting wild onions and Polk salad from vacant yards, were more than expeditions for sustenance; they were lessons in the abundance of nature. She showed us beauty in the overlooked and wisdom in the seemingly ordinary.

The building on Rosa Parks and Eighth Avenue North, with its peculiar sulfur water, epitomized the depths of my mother's belief in the extraordinary. While the world might have turned its nose away from the pungent aroma, she recognized the potential within its depths. In her eyes, it was more than just water; it was a metaphor for life's challenges – a reminder that there often lies the seed of improvement within seemingly unfavorable circumstances. She instilled in us the courage to look beyond the surface, to find value where others saw none.

With its lively hues and delightful summer tunes, Kool-Aid stood as a testament to my mother's knack for instilling delight into even the simplest of joys. As she blended the powder and swirled the mixture, she was fashioning more than a revitalizing drink; she was sculpting instances of togetherness and friendship. Those shared sips and laughter-infused afternoons surpassed mere thirst-quenching; they nurtured bonds.

Our cherished customs weren't mere phrases; they embodied my mother's sagacity. "Operation Kool-Aid" taught the art of striking the perfect equilibrium – a gentle nudge that life's sweetness requires thoughtful adjustment. And "Project Kool-Aid" was a whispered encouragement to endure life's challenges with unwavering strength. These sayings were her gifts to us, encoded with life lessons that would guide us through the trials and tribulations that lay ahead.

My mother's legacy wasn't just in her teachings and actions. She was a master at turning adversity into opportunity, making the scarcity of our circumstances into the abundance of our potential.

I never could imagine how she did all of that. Now, as an adult, the one thing that comes to mind is perseverance and resilience.

Yup, that's my Mama!

The Flight to Freedom

~Chapter 3~

'The Community That Cared'

One cannot survive without the solidarity of one's community.

Trina Frierson

I grew up surrounded by love. I count myself as one of the blessed ones. I fondly remember my time with my family, but I didn't just have blood relations to fall back on. The neighborhood I grew up in was full of kind, supportive, and loving people who always loved our family.

Mama always had a helping hand, ready to take the load off her burdened shoulders whenever needed. She was always thankful and kept reminding us to be grateful, too.

All the families on the street built strong bonds with one another. It was beautiful to see people who could be labeled as strangers come together, hand in hand, ready to help their neighbor. I felt engulfed by a protective shield, wrapping up and keeping me from harm's way. Relationships are essential for survival, and the most supportive relationships are built with your community, which you call yours. It's your home.

My fondest memories of my time with my community are linked to the Cleveland Community Center. It was a part of our itinerary for years. Throughout the week, mornings from Monday to Friday were set in stone. They all started with Mama's cooking. Even our German Shepard waddled into the house in time for Mama's food. His name was Tiger, and he was quite a unique dog.

I remember people only came into the house if one of us walked them through. That's because Tiger loved to grab visitors' ankles and bite them if he wasn't familiar with their scent. He was a fluffy bundle of joy and the best guard dog one could ask for. I used to put on my rolling skates and get behind him, holding his collar while he pulled me down the middle of the street. I adored skating at the Cleveland Center. We had this skating ritual first, then enjoyed a dance at the center.

Those were the golden days. Even the bad times seemed fun to reminisce about, like when I got caught eating at my friend's house by my brother Gerald. I liked to call him BaBa. Throughout my childhood, BaBa bullied me in more ways than anyone can imagine, but this particular day, he told me, *"If you get me some, I won't tell Mama."*

So, I asked my friend's mother if my brother could have some food, too. Due to the wonderful community engagement, or us being Southerners, she said yes. That allowed me to add another secret to the books.

This was around the summer when mom was held up at work, and the community center had not initiated its free lunch program. Usually, when Mama was busy, we were at the Cleveland Community Center, where they planned a day of fun activities. These activities ranged from swimming, sports, boy and girl scouts, and arts and crafts. You name it, and they had it for all the kids in the community. That was our daycare. We usually gathered on the sidewalk at the corner of North 5th Street when we weren't at the center.

Most of the parents in the neighborhood were aware that if their kids were not at home, the first place to call was the Cleveland Community Center. It was indeed our home away from home. I woke up early to head to the community center, but only after stopping by Mrs. Louis Jackson's house. I loved going to her because she was the designated candy lady in the neighborhood. You could buy penny candy at her house instead of going to E & W Market. Her house was a couple of houses down from the community center.

My favorite sports were basketball and swimming during the summer. After spending so much time at the pool, I eventually became a part of the swim team and a certified lifeguard. During these days, I could never find enough girls who played basketball, and I ended up being the only girl on the team sometimes. I recall playing against my brother BaBa, whom I was once intimidated by until my other brother, Freddie, told me, *"Always play to win, no matter who it is, including your brother."*

That day finally came. I beat BaBa not only at one game but several, and that jumpstarted my motivation to become a great basketball player.

During middle school, I didn't have much pressure on me from the other kids, except for the fact that I was always one of the biggest kids in class. Most people were intimidated by my size, but once they got to know me, they knew all they could see was my body's size, not my heart's. I get this a lot from people today, too! They see me and make judgments just from what they can tell about my size rather than who I truly am. Yet, they dance to a different tune when they get to know me or hear about me and my work.

Due to my size, I remember being accused of bullying, but I never acted on it. One day, I was called to the office at Glenn Elementary School on Cleveland St., and the principal claimed that I threatened to beat up a girl named Mary. I was shocked! Later, I found out that my friend, Lena, threatened Mary, and she was too afraid to reveal her name, so she used my name instead. I wasn't a perfect child, but fighting was not my thing unless I had to. In fact, as a child, I can recall only three fights in school or on the playground.

Now, when it comes to arguments, I may have had a dozen or two. That's because we went from a community that promoted resolution. If our parents found out we were part of a disagreement, they would bring us to each other's houses, making us best friends again. Back then, parents always found a way to gather us all to make the best of things.

My community pushed me to be the best version of myself. I began working at a young age because all my brothers and sisters were working. It seemed like the only time I could see my family was late at night. My youngest brother, next to me, started working when he was 15, washing the dishes at the Piccadilly restaurant and Shoney Big Boy. Between 12 and 16, I went to school and looked forward to spending the summer at the community center. Working and playing basketball were my highlights of the summer.

However, I remember being forced to go to vacation bible school. I eventually started to like it and began singing in the Cleveland Street Missionary Baptist Church choir in my white blouse and blue skirt. When it came to church, I hung out with a different group of people. At the age of 12, I was baptized at the same church. We began attending that church after my oldest brother, Herschel, met his girlfriend, whom he later married, and they had a child together. Before attending Cleveland Street Baptist, my mom used a taxi to get us to the 15th Ave Baptist Church every Sunday. I never recalled her serving on any of the committees, but she was present every Sunday.

When I was a teenager, between the ages of 15 and 17, I experienced my second session of smoking weed on my walk to school with my cousins who lived up the street from us. We all walked to junior high school together, and if we missed a day, we would come to the other's house to ask why we weren't on the walk to school that day. My brother and I went to the same school, Highland Heights, but he didn't walk with us. He built his identity and found a group of guys to hang with. By then, I had gained courage from walking and smoking a toke at different places, and by summer, I found myself meeting up with a new group of friends in the park at the community center to smoke weed and drink Old English 800 beer.

One of the girls in the group could go to the store and get a beer because back then, parents could send you to the store and get it, and they knew it was for the parents. But this girl would grab two quarts of beer for us, the cups, and the bag of weed. We only had to bring our dollars to her, and we could party on the covered sliding board at the park. This went on until I was 16 years old.

One evening, when it had turned dark, I was walking home with my friends, smoking a cigarette, and my mom was on the porch. You could sit on our front porch and see me crossing the hill from the community center. I denied it, and she said, *"I saw what I saw, and I don't appreciate you making me out to be a liar! You never had to lie to me about anything. Why now?"*

I eventually told her the truth. My mom never whipped me, although when she threatened to, I would cry as if she had whipped me for hours. While she never beat me, my oldest brother Herschel did. It resulted in me walking home from school with the same group. His best friend lived on Meridian, which crossed Douglas Avenue, where Highland Heights Junior High School was. He saw me smoking and reported it to my brother, and as soon as my brother got off work, he came home and started right into me. He said,

"You think you're old enough to smoke. Do you want to smoke instead of playing basketball?"

I remember that evening, after getting whipped, he made me clean the whole house. I'm talking about a five-bedroom house that was not cleaned at all. It was a house where dishes were piled up, clothes were strewn everywhere, and trash was overrun. This resulted from us not cleaning up during the week while mom worked two jobs, and every time she asked why we hadn't cleaned, my excuse was that I had homework or practice. She was a trustworthy caretaker in her own right. After that eye-opener from being whipped by my brother, I knew he was the father figure missing from my life because my father died when I was six.

Regardless of my father's absence, I never felt abandoned. I was raised not just by the strongest woman in the world but also by the most loving community.

"One of the marvelous things about community is that it enables us to welcome and help people in a way we couldn't as individuals. When we pool our strength and share the work and responsibility, we can welcome many

people, even those in deep distress, and perhaps help them find self-confidence and inner healing." **- Jean Vanier**

~Chapter 4~

'My Ethics at an Early Age'

Being a family means you are a part of something very wonderful. It means you will love and be loved for the rest of your life.

Lisa Weed

Independence is a tricky thing. I craved it when I was young. The power to do anything I wanted whenever I pleased. The freedom to make my own decisions. Like any other teenager, I believed that my independence would begin with a stable source of income. So, I started working from a very early age.

Since I began working at a young age, I could only see my family late at night. The time I spent with my family was very precious, and to this day, I hold it very dear to my heart. It was an exciting experience to venture into the professional world at such a young age. It was new and exciting, but at the same time, I felt out of place. Hustle is the right word to describe that period of my life.

My mornings were spent in classes, and my afternoons were consumed by basketball. It's funny how busy I was, but my youthful mind never felt the burden. I was never too tired and always made time for fun with my friends and family.

I guess that was my biggest support—my community. I often wonder if we will ever see a community like this again, where families were a united front, even when they were not blood related. These were the times when it didn't matter what your economic status, who dressed the best, or whether your house was fancy. In our community, love was at the top of the agenda. Even in new experiences, I had familiar faces surrounding me, so it was easier to become accustomed to things. I always felt safe. I also always felt like my mother had her eyes on me, even when she wasn't physically there, which was entertaining in its own way.

As the years passed, I went from junior high school to high school, with basketball at the top of my agenda. I began playing basketball in 9th grade in 1979 at Maplewood High School. This was the first-year 9th grade was integrated with 10-12th graders in high school. Becoming the best player on the team was at the top of my list. It was a priority. And there was just as much support from teachers and coaches as in my community. My two favorite teachers, Mrs. Jennings, and Mrs. Howard, along with Coach Martin, Coach Hickman, and Coach Gamble, were more than just doing their job as teachers and coaches for me. They were like extended family. I can remember being in middle school and playing basketball.

I tackled all of that with an after-school job at the age of twelve. I started my career working at the Winfrey Corner store (E & W). I was very grateful for this opportunity, and all my thanks went to Thomas Walker, who encouraged Winfrey, the store owner, to hire me. Thomas was one of the kids who were a part of the community. Winfrey took him under his wing and later adopted him as his son. Thomas was his only son.

This opportunity was another reason I felt so blessed to be a part of such a tightly knit community. If it weren't for Vernon Winfrey, I would never have been able to work at such a young age. That was an experience that taught me so much, and it truly transformed my outlook on my future. I'm genuinely grateful for Vernon Winfrey, who was a true pillar in the community. Winfrey held our community together through his work as a businessman. He was very crafty in how he expanded his business. He owned two staple centers of the community: the corner store and Winfrey's barbershop. The best lesson I learned from him, among several others, was ethics. I learned how to discipline myself under the guise of a strict and resilient work ethic, which was an extremely valuable lesson.

My experience at the corner store empowered me and taught me how to appreciate and empower others. Now that I look back on it, that's precisely what Mr. Winfrey did for me. He showed me that someone's family or background did not define their place in our community. Everyone was equal and received equal love and respect from every other member.

I started to see my community in a different light. It only increased my love for those who supported my mother and family. Mr. Winfrey's beliefs greatly inspired me. He firmly advocated embracing our responsibility to support our fellow people. He made me see that it was our job to offer a hand to the less fortunate and help them rise to a more respectable position, regardless of their circumstances.

Mr. Winfrey left a legacy with me, and I wanted to pass it on and use it to make a mark in this world. The core of Mr. Winfrey's legacy was to, *"LOVE without Permission."*

Unsurprisingly, Winfrey ran for an eight-year term as the councilman for our district. And it is not an exaggeration to claim that he excelled at it. He provided a healthy community store for families to access groceries conveniently and allowed kids to work and make a sustainable living for themselves. Besides seeing my mom go to work every day, rain or shine, Winfrey gave me my work ethic. I started by making $10.00 a day, and by the time I turned 21, I was making $20.00 a day. My responsibilities at the start of my journey at the corner store included stocking the inventory and bagging the items at the cash register. Once I polished my skills in those departments, I started getting calls from the store to ask if I could come in for work at the last minute. Of course, I couldn't refuse because working in that space allowed me to understand how customer service worked. It also developed my communication skills while interacting with new people, which was a skill that assisted me throughout my life.

My mom always said, *"Look a person in their eyes when you speak or communicate. "*Her words helped me in my professional life while working at the store.

My work at the corner store for Mr. Winfrey gave me a sense of pride, and you could see that on my face as I strutted down my neighborhood's street in east Nashville. I felt special because while the other kids my age enjoyed their lives, playing outside, fooling around, and going on vacations with their families, I found joy in working and helping around the house.

I recall how simple life used to be. I can buy dinner and snacks from the store for only $5.00! I remember purchasing some bologna, cheese, bread, Kool-Aid, and counter cookies, which were stacked in a big jar, and they were the first things you saw when you entered the store.

Those delights only cost me a penny! The affordability of that time helped me save a lot of money.

I recall saving a week's pay from the store to enjoy myself in downtown Nashville. I remember making **$10.00 a day**, and by the time I had $100 bucks saved up, I thought I was rich. It was a massive accomplishment for a twelve-year-old. I remember the first time I bought myself a pair of Levi jeans and a printed T-shirt. It was an empowering experience to take care of myself at such a young age, but my biggest relief came from taking a load off my mother, who was constantly worrying about caring for her babies.

It was a pleasure to be able to give her a hand. She worked her life away to provide us with the best opportunities. She was always my role model. This is the lady who often smiles through her pain. You would notice it when she ended her workday and prepared her family for the next day. Tough skin and a big heart with a glowing spirit that reflected rays of sunshine while only standing at 5 feet 4 inches.

I never knew what my mother went through until my latter parenting days. In the times when I was lost as a parent, I would imagine reflections of my mother and say to myself, *"What would Mama do?"*

One of the first things that always came to mind was perseverance. I couldn't understand why she never gave up in the rough times, but I know now that she prayed through much of it as her load became heavy. Why did she love us equally? It was because we were taught independently, mainly by our dreams and goals. She wanted us to be ourselves yet love one another unconditionally. It created a powerful bond among us siblings.

One of the things that I saw my brother, Baba, do in junior high was sell candy. Seeing him do that generated an idea that I could also do it. So, I started selling candy to make some extra money. At that time, I had never heard the word residual income. Sometimes, at night, my brother and I would gather around the table to count how much we made and then figure out ways to make more by purchasing more candy with our profits.

One night, I came home, and my brother had way more money than someone who sold candy would make, and I struggled to understand how that was possible. That was when I began questioning whether the candy of sale was for me. Later, I found out that he was selling more than just candy. He had taken the leap from candy to weed.

Yes, he had the upper hand on me, and I had to decide whether I wanted to take that risk or be the successful basketball player that I had intended to be in the first place. At that time, I refused to follow in his footsteps. Finding out that my brother was selling weed was shocking at first. But then, I slowly became terrified of losing him to the prison system. Once that system gets a hold of you, it chews you up and spits you out.

As a kid, I saw his ability to go to the store and buy whatever he wanted at any time as exciting. But it was a misleading thought. I glorified his financial independence without knowing how dark the consequences could be. At the time, I never even imagined that I could sell drugs, so I decided to stick to candy of sale. Because during that time, the simple joys of life were enough for me.

Baba was next to the youngest sibling, making me the baby of the family. My four brothers were like night and day. My eldest brother, Herschel, was as precious to me as my mother. But he was considered the oldest man in the family after my father's passing, and we all looked up to him. He had the coolest fashion style back then. I'm talking about bell-bottom pants and stacks, the shoes with heels that the men wore back in the day. He also worked two jobs—one for Metro and the other for the State of Tennessee at age 20. He even assisted my mother in helping me with anything that I needed for school, including a lot of my basketball gear. I still recall wanting new shoes; he always came through for me.

On the day I received disciplinary action from my brother for smoking a cigarette while walking home from junior high school with my friends, I still recall the nicotine buzz I got along the way. I knew our community was genuinely connected from one block to another, but I didn't think someone five blocks away would recognize me at 2 p.m., coming from school while smoking. I thought they would be at work like my mom was. My brother's best friend was watching the 2 o'clock dismal and just happened to see me taking a draw off the cigarette before passing it to my friend. That's when my brother Herschel showed up as my father. As soon as I got home, he came to the house and asked the question, *"So, you think you grown? You smoke now?"*

And, of course, I lied. He reminded me that his friend had no reason to lie after pulling off his belt and whipping me. That was the time he made me clean the entire house.

That wasn't enough to stop me from smoking, but I never smoked in the school zone again...

Around this age, I rarely spoke about weed, but this was when my sister gave me my first joint. From there, my experience took flight. I found myself drinking a little when I got to Maplewood High School. It was just part of the culture that came with being on the team, and the ones who didn't drink were looked at as a square. As I finished my first year, I entered my sophomore year, and that was the start of one of the most challenging times of my life. I did not know it then, but this year marked the beginning of the events that fueled most of my childhood trauma. Nothing could have prepared me for what was to come. It all came together and hit me like a freight train. I was left emotionally bruised and beaten.

It all started with the death of my older brother, who was my only father figure. He was the glue that held our family together.

I was unprepared for the night when my mother and I sat in her room eating a bowl of homemade chili. It's still as vivid as it was yesterday. My mom was sitting in her chair, and I was sitting on the floor beside her when a loud, frantic knock pounded on the door. The barks of our dog, Tiger, grew louder. Upon answering the door, we saw a gentleman named Dwight who lived a street over. He was the candy lady's son. *He was the one who brought us the news of Herschel being shot!*

It was unbelievable because my brother was at work and my mother had just spoken to him earlier. What was unbelievable came true. He was shot while on duty by a guy considered his friend. They had been close and shared several activities like most friends. That night, something had transpired between them, causing an altercation, and when my brother got the best of him, he pulled his weapon as a security officer and shot my brother in the chest. This was not only traumatic because he died, but he happened to work at the same hospital as my mother and my other brothers.

This was hard on my mom; we had lost the anchor of our family. I knew I had my mother, but somehow, my eldest brother made our family complete. He was my mother's biggest support. As time passed, I became withdrawn and lacked interest in my daily routines, including school and sports.

My sister, the oldest of six siblings, began to suffer from a mental illness. Back then, we did not know what to call it. We witnessed her talking to herself and making decisions that were not practical. This was very strange coming from a woman who was well put together and successfully working with News Channel 5. She was traveling and known to be the smartest in the family.

It seemed that my brother's death took more than his life. Our family was genuinely robbed of more than his death. To this day, my sister is lost with an untreated illness. She ended up becoming a part of the homeless community. She went missing from Tennessee, and we didn't find her until twenty years later, bed-ridden in LA with many unanswered questions for our family.

Later, my mom was diagnosed with colon cancer. When I look back at how our family was affected by my brother's death, I see it as a true tragedy.

As we grew close, we tried to fill his shoes. But at the end of the day, the shoes of Hershel were too big to conquer.

Freddy, who became the eldest, was full of anger and resentment. He fought through most situations after having too many drinks. He would later become murdered on our front porch months after my mother passed.

Kenny was the mellow, smooth, do-what-you-gotta-do child and never caused Mama any problems. He would be the brother you could talk to, and he would listen more than talk but always come back with a great suggestion.

BaBa was the child who always had a good or bad hustle. He was the one child that kept my Mama up at night. And no matter what BaBa did, she loved her son, and would always try to point him in the right direction, yet never gave up on him. You could never force her to lose her love for her kids.

~Chapter 5~

'The Beginning of My Faith'

Faith is a tricky word. It's a word with many meanings, each with a different context.

It's an amalgamation of letters that hold so much power and truth within them that saying it feels heavy on your tongue. A bit like saying love. Or death. Such a heavy, *heavy* word.

Some people see it as a sack of stones tied to their feet, dragging them further down in an ocean of their own mistakes- and shame. Others see it as an escape from the monsters that keep them up at night, snarling their teeth from the dark corner. But I see it as something you cling to for hope.

I hope that you will find your path—a path that is free of pain, loss, and sorrow.

Faith is an invisible string that attaches to your heart, clinging until its last string unravels. It's a rock that grounds you yet lift you from the darkest pits of despair.

Everyone has faith in their heart, whether attached to a religion, their spirit, or the universe.

It can be for God, Karma, Providence, even yourself or a loved one—but we all have faith. It takes many forms, but its rudimentary essence remains the same throughout to help you find the right way. The actual path, the way to Nirvana, the way to peace. And fulfillment.

You might have taken a wrong turn somewhere and found yourself completely lost in a forest of horrors. Life's never-ending twists and turns might leave you in the middle of nowhere with no hope of finding your way back. Life consists of long journeys, and losing our way is so easy.

I've lost my way so many times, but that essence of hope in my heart directed me back. No matter how far I wandered, I always found my way back home. My journey with faith started very early.

At the ripe age of 12, I encountered that string of hope that people cling to, but it was just the beginning of my tumultuous journey, and I lost my grip on that string a few times. From 12 to 16, I focused on schoolwork and daydreamed about summer.

Working at the Winfrey corner store and playing basketball was the highlight of my day. But then, before I knew it, I was being forced to go to vacation bible school. Initially, I dreaded it. I thought I would be bored, and I would rather play basketball. But eventually, I started liking it and became a part of the Cleveland Street Missionary Baptist Church choir. I never knew I could sing before others, but I soon found my place in the singing group.

I remember standing on the podium with my pristine white blouse and navy-blue skirt. I had my group of friends, but the people I found at church differed significantly. It was an opportunity to interact and bond with new people, who taught me much of what I know today. They became a part of my community. I still remember the time I was baptized. I was only 12 years old.

I was submerged in the water and too young to realize the depth of the action. The feeling of the smooth water

rippled over my skin. I can still remember it all so clearly. Before attending the Cleveland Street Baptist, I participated at the 15th Avenue Baptist Church. My mom used a taxi to get us to church every Sunday.
I can't remember her serving on any of the committees, but she was there every Sunday.

　　We never missed church. The 15th Ave Church was somewhat of a blur, but I recall my mother loading the younger three siblings up in a white taxicab in front of the house. Back then, you could call a cab and schedule a ride, or you had a favorite driver who kept you on the Sunday schedule. Most of my memories revolve around how excited my mom was on Sunday to serve the Lord and how she would listen to one of the radio stations that still airs today, WVOL.

　　On Sunday mornings, I always expected gospel music to boom through the speaker of the taxi, and one of the voices I still recall was gospel singer Bobby Jones! I remember being star-struck when I noticed him across the street at our neighbor's house. My mom brought us in from church, and by the time we got home, family and friends were awaiting to chow down on her Southern cooking. Sundays were a wholesome experience, and I always look back at my memories of such days with such fondness. The entire community came together under one roof for a single purpose. It united us more than we already were. We truly felt enriched in each other's company under the bright sun of Sunday mornings. Eating together at our home was another beautiful experience.

My magnificent mother would cook for the entire community, and not a single crumb would be left on their plates.

The church was not my only encounter with faith. Even though it lasted only a week in June during summer break, vacation bible school left another mark on me. I wasn't bored in the slightest.

It was the kind of place where you would go, and the elders would make it fun while they taught you about the church's history and the bible verses, and there was always a meal afterward.

My mom ensured I was at vacation bible school and the junior choir, where we were mandated to wear blue skirts and white blouses. Mrs. Sally Blair made our blue skirts and easter dresses for the choir. She was a sweet lady, and I loved trying on the dresses she sewed for all the girls in the choir.

To this day, I don't have a voice that's made for singing. I don't have the soft timbre that rumbles through your ears as it plays with the notes and the lyrics of an ensemble of music.

But somehow, they allowed me to be a part of the choir and trained me to fit in like a real singer. At the week's end, we would devise a skit. Our group leader would call us every night to ensure we knew our part. It was strange that my mom ensured I was in bible school, but my brothers never had to attend.

I had gotten used to the fact that we were not all treated equally as her kids. It was a subtle, sad wave of acceptance that I couldn't deny any longer. I always thought our mother never differentiated between her kids, but these memories make me realize that I'm looking at things through a rose-tinted glass.

But my experience at this church began my journey with faith. I recall going to church Sunday after Sunday. One day after, the preacher said, *"The doors of the church are open.* You may come by Christian experience or by baptism." Something inside of me switched. That thread of hope strengthened, tangled around my beating heart, and attached to my soul.

That string led my tiny feet down the aisle and asked for baptism. The pastor asked me, "Do you understand what you are doing?" To which I replied, "Yes, I want to give my life to Christ."

My mom poured her eyes out. Her happy tears streamed down her face. I understood what giving my life to Christ would mean. The other members congratulated me and invited me to the new members' class. These were the good old days. I even recall a member talking to my mom from the pulpit,

"Mrs. Frierson, don't worry about her. We got her, and *we promise to take care of her* at Cleveland Street Church."

Her words echoed in my head. I knew these words were supposed to comfort my mom, but they felt like a tight embrace around my small body, protecting me. I felt safe. I was surrounded by those I loved and those who loved me back.

This was when I grabbed that string. The anchor. The compass that would lead me out of the dark forest time and time again. The string that would never let go, no matter how far I strayed. It tightened, strained, and withered, but it never unraveled itself from around my heart. It was as adamant as the day I dunked my body in the water at 12. All the wrong turns I took blended into the sands of time as I grabbed onto that hope. I clenched my shaky fingers around it and emerged from the dark corner with my head held high.

The first time I found my faith was at the Cleveland Street Church, and it stayed with me for the rest of my life.

~Chapter 6~

'Experimenting with the Unknown'

The rising smoke.
The pungent smell.
My buzzing fingertips.
The heaviness in my chest.
Staring down the mouth of a bottle.
An encounter that happened all too soon.

***

My first encounter with alcohol was when I was 15 years old. I was quite young to be drinking, but it didn't feel like a gateway to a spiral at the time. I was just having some fun with my friends. Surprisingly, my encounter with smoking weed happened sooner than that.

Looking back at these experiences, I pondered why I indulged in such activities. After years of wondering, I still haven't found the answer. There was no concrete driving force. No factor to blame. I fell into bad habits. I got a taste, and I liked how it made me feel. I was young and foolish. I thought the buzz and the numbing pain made me a better version of myself. My adolescent and irrational brain believed that the burn of alcohol and the cotton mouth after a long puff was the way of life. It made everything less bleak. Less painful. Less terrifying.

It was fun and exciting. I felt like I was at the top of the world. Nothing could come in the way of my euphoric state. But it only lasted until the buzz went away. And with the years passing, the duration of the buzz just kept increasing. Until it was too late to turn back, that 15-year-old girl didn't realize how quickly it turned so dark. But that little girl would be proud of where I am today. I found a way out of that darkness that engulfed and scared her. I hid her from the lurking monsters and kept her safe. The way I turned around, left the bottle, found peace, and found God, would make that little girl very proud.

I wasn't the kindest to myself as I battled with life's woes. I made mistakes, but I found a way to rectify them. This story. My story. My experiences. They all shaped who I am today, and I am not ashamed of them. As a child, I delved into the unknown without much thought. But the rash jumps caught up to me as I aged. The dark abyss that I unknowingly slipped into became larger and more menacing. The quicksand trapped my feet. The more I struggled, the more I sank. And I kept dropping until the thick captor was up to my nose. But just as my breath was about to be taken away, I found a rope to pull me out. And I held on for dear life because I didn't want to drown. I wanted to survive. I wanted to be better. I wanted to change.

And I did. Which is why I'm telling my story. With the hope that this will become someone else's rope to pull them out of the thick quicksand. Something that they can hold on to for dear life. I thought my journey started with a beer, but now that I think about it, it started with weed. I was 14 years old at the time.

I recall that moment very clearly. My mother had gone to work for the day. My sister and some of my brothers ended up smoking weed in her bedroom, which was next to the kitchen. At the time, I just sat around and watched. During this time, they talked and planned their day, often daydreaming about what they wanted to achieve. At least one of them continually asked if I had a basketball game, and if I did, they would say, *"Have a good game."*

I sat on the sidelines in this old brown flowered printed chair and watched them smoke. Of course, they didn't feel the need to let me participate, but I remember them letting my 16-year-old brother have a few puffs from time to time. So, one day I guess my sister felt terrible that I was always in the room but not participating. I would look at them earnestly, and they could tell I wanted to participate in the activity. She decided to give me a joint when no one was around.

Back then, we had the old TOP rolling papers, which would roll better than a machine. It's safe to say that Brenda was a perfectionist in her own right. It was not as perfect as the ones I watched them smoke, but it had enough weed dust to make me feel like a part of it. Her only request was, *"Don't tell no one."* And, of course, I said, *"Ok."*

During the ages of 15 and 17, I experienced my second session of smoking weed on a walk to school with my cousins who lived up the street from us. We all walked to junior high school together, and if we missed a day, we came to the other's house to ask why we weren't on the walk to school that day. My brother and I went to the same school, Highland Heights, but he didn't walk with us. He had gained his own identity and found a separate group of guys to hang with.

I remember drinking my first beer and not feeling a buzz; it gave me a relaxing feeling, and I thought I was somewhat grown up. I sneaked the first drink from the dinner table but then found out that my friends in the neighborhood were drinking and meeting up at the park, and I remember drinking a couple of cups of beer with them. When I finished, I found myself going to sleep. I don't recall getting drunk until I got to my senior year. My friend and I, Jermone, graduated together. He had his dad's car, and we went around that evening just partying until we threw up. It was a crazy day, but we survived!

At this time, recreational drugs were not popular around my neighborhood. I had heard of weed and heroin, but I had done enough of the "Just say No to Drugs" program at the community center that I believed, at that time, that they were genuinely deadly.

My first few experiences seemed like trivial contacts, but they opened a deathly door for me. Looking back, I realize that I was much too young. Perhaps, my company wasn't the best. But I can't blame my mistakes on others. I was a child, but I continued to make the same decisions. Now, I realize that my choices don't define me. I try every day to be a better version of myself. But this was only the beginning. I would have to face more giant monsters than a can of Old English 800 beer.

~Chapter 7~

'My Father Figure'

An angel snatched away too soon.
A young man's shoulders carry such heavy burdens.
His protection was my anchor.
His strong presence was my shield.
The image of a father.
Residing in my heart till the end of time.
My loving older brother,
Herschel.
***

When people think of an ideal image of a home, they imagine a mother, a father, and their children. They think of a passionate, emotional, and caring mother. They imagine the father as a strong protector who stands before his family like a metal shield. The mother is the caretaker of the home. She raises her children with love and compassion, teaching them to grow up to be good people. The father raises his kids to be strong and independent. He teaches them how to navigate life's complicated and narrow alleys, meandering easily and gracefully. The two of them build a home together, supporting one another and sharing the burdens of life.

The children are surrounded by love. They're safe. They're happy.

But my image of an ideal home was different. It wasn't as if I wasn't happy, or I didn't feel loved. Quite the opposite. An incredible mother raised me, and the love of our community surrounded me. The only difference is that I didn't have a father.

My mother took up both jobs. She didn't have anyone to share the burden with. She would care for the home and raise her children with love and compassion while teaching them how to navigate life and grow up to be independent and strong. She did it all by herself. And not once did I ever feel like my home lacked.

I had a very wholesome childhood. There's this emphasis on having a father or something akin to one in your formative years, but I grew up without one. My older brother Herschel was the closest thing to a father in my home. He was my mother's support in all aspects of life. Herschel encompassed all the qualities one might search for in a father figure, and I was truly blessed to have him by my side.

My older brother was strict. It wasn't like Herschel was a mean man. He was as precious as my mother; he was the oldest man in the family, and we looked up to him. My siblings and I were always very close to one another. Our mother raised us always to love each other, no matter what. And Herschel was the best example of that. Even when he got upset and punished us for messing up, we knew he was doing the right thing. I remember when he punished me for smoking. At first, I was troubled by the idea of cleaning our entire house, but at the end of the day, I knew he was doing it in my best interest. His stronghold was a huge help for my mother, who could spare some time and focus on her job at the hospital to keep the house running.

When Herschel got old enough, he even contributed to household finances. Bit by bit, he took the load off Mama. He worked two jobs—one for Metro and the other for the State of Tennessee at 20 years old. Herschel was responsible with all of his duties, and I honestly looked up to him as the perfect image of who I wanted to become. He started working at a young age and earned enough to support himself. It was truly remarkable. He was my motivation—my inspiration.

He assisted my mother in helping me with anything I needed for school, including a lot of my basketball gear. He bought me new shoes whenever I needed them, especially when I wore mine out after playing too much basketball. It was like someone in the background always had my back, rain, or shine. Herschel would be standing there. Ready to help me with anything I needed.

That was my idea of what a father should be like. But it was snatched away from me all too soon. Herschel was the father figure and the glue to help hold the family together. That glue eroded that dark night he lost his life in the boiler room of the General Hospital.

That night is burned into my brain like an awful itch. Something that tingles from the inside, and you can't get to it no matter how much you scratch. It stays and festers until you learn to live with the constant reminder that it's still inside you, right under your skin.

The knock that startled my mother and me at 9 p.m. still echoes in my ears. Mama's face when she heard the news of his death from his friend is still fresh in my memory. The pain. The terror. The disbelief. Just like that, our home was broken. Shattered. The glue had dissipated.

She had looked at Herschel's friend with a confused look. The erratic conversation that transpired after that plays on repeat in my head, *"No, baby, Herschel is at work!"* Herschel's friend replied, "I know they've been trying to call you." She said, *"My phone didn't ring!"* *"It's ringing busy,"* he countered.

As we looked at the phone, we were gutted to see it was lying beside the unplugged couch. *"They're sending a car to get you now,"* he added. My Mama started putting on her clothes, and I followed suit. The drive to the hospital seemed like a fever dream. Blurry, long, unclear. The traffic lights were jumping around, and my head was spinning. I was queasy and dissociative. I felt like someone had reached down my throat, grabbed my stomach, and plunged it out with their fist.

By the time we arrived at the hospital, all we could encounter were heartbreaking words, *"We did all we could do, Mrs. Frierson."* And that was that.

Like that, the glue, the support system, and my father figure were stolen from my family and me. We were left stranded. Fallen as the rug that was pulled from under our feet slipped away. It happened so fast. Nobody saw it coming.

This traumatic event did a couple of things to me. I realized what a pillar my brother was in the community. I could see it at his funeral. So many of his friends, family, and loved ones showed up to bid him farewell. It was indeed a heartwarming sight. There was barely any room inside the venue, and some people had to stand outside because the large church could not hold more bodies.

The other thing was that I slipped into severe depression. The worst part was that I was so young that I didn't even know what depression was. I spent most of my sophomore year at home, and I only passed my exams by the grace of God. I felt like everything in my life had lost its meaning.

All the colors had drained out, leaving a dull filter of grey and black. I couldn't find joy in anything. Not even in school, with my friends, at the community center, or playing basketball. Everything seemed like a drag. I felt like a ship without an anchor, floating off into the sea with no direction. I was so lost. I felt alone. It was like I was sinking in a pool of thick black tar. Pure darkness engulfed me, and for the longest time, I couldn't find my way back to the light. That year, my head was always somewhere else. I was detached from my body. I remember taking long walks in a complete trance. My feet would move of their own volition, and when I came to my senses, I realized how far away I had walked from home.

Herschel's loss changed me. It bruised me so profoundly that, to this day, the wound aches. It throbs and bleeds.

He lives in my heart, and even if he left too soon, he lives on in my memories. Memories of his smile. His laugh. And his immense love for his family.

~Chapter 8~

'Finding Purpose After Trauma'

Long sleepless nights.
A heavy feeling of ever-present despair.
The feeling of black quicksand pulling me in.
Stuck in the substance with no way out.
A hand reaches upwards.
There's still some fight left in me.

***

When we experience something that leaves us shattered and broken, we feel there's no way out.

The aftermath of a traumatic event leaves you numb. Lethargic. Exhausted.

Something keeps pulling you down; before you know it, the darkness has reached your nose.

This is a crucial point.

This is where you decide whether to let that darkness engulf you whole until you're out of air or if you're willing to fight one last time and force yourself out from underneath the weight of your fears.

I leaned toward the first of those choices at a point in my life.

After my brother Herschel was snatched from us, I was in utter misery. I felt like all the light in my life had dimmed into thick darkness. I had never known loss like that and ultimately gave up on myself. I was stuck in bed for days on end, unable to focus on anything I used to adore. I was barely attending school, which took a toll on my education. All I wanted to do the year after Herschel's death was lay in one spot until my bones dissolved into the mattress, until I disappeared and never encountered the pain and suffering of losing a loved one, my father figure.

At the time, I didn't know what depression was, so I didn't think of going to therapy or getting help for what I was experiencing. It was a lot for a young girl. But I was so lucky to have my friends and cousins as a support system that pulled me out of that menacing darkness. They managed to help me get back to living. I realized I could mourn somebody else's life, but that didn't mean I should mourn the life I was blessed with. I had to keep on living. You can't die without someone. You can be sad, hurt, and in pain, and feeling all those negative emotions is okay. But you can't forget that you have your own life to live. I had to continue living on this earth and I couldn't take that for granted.

My friends and family reminded me that my brother would have wanted me to go on and be all I could be. Herschel always pushed me to be my best self and knew I would do great things. He kept telling me to take the leap and try new things because that was the only way forward. His words of wisdom became my mantra. This realization was a gateway to my reintroduction to my real passion, my love for basketball. The feeling I got as I strode across the cement flooring and jumped with the back of my heels to shoot the ball through a hoop was exhilarating. It made me feel alive, and that's exactly what I needed to feel. I recalled how Herschel always supported my dream of becoming a professional basketball player, and I used that as a crutch to start playing again.

I was reminded of how proud he was of me, especially on the basketball court. I tried out for the varsity team when I returned to Maplewood High School for my junior year. Six seniors were on the team, and they were all amazing, like all-star-level amazing. But I found myself just as good by making backup as a six-man. It was Patricia and I who rotated for the six-man spot. She got more start times than me, but my skills allowed me to align with them. Those were the good days. I was intimated by the other players surrounding me on the field, and I was discouraged for a second. What if I was better than I thought I was? What if I had lost my skill? What if the break I took from playing destroyed all my chances of making it on the field?

But I didn't let those nagging thoughts overcome the reason why I started playing again. To make Herschel proud. I used that as my driving force. My inspiration. My motivation. And before I knew it, I got the charm back. As I entered my senior year, I became the basketball team captain. It was a dream come true. I felt like I had finally grasped something I had been working on my entire life. I was not the smartest in my senior class. I remember having a graduation class of 309 students, and my number, according to my grades, fell in the low 300's. Although I was not the brightest, I loved playing basketball. Because of basketball, I earned a scholarship to play in college. The sport was my savior during one of the most challenging times of my life. And because of this amazing experience, I could go to college and build the life Herschel wanted.

I was my team's city, state, regional, and MVP in 1982. It was indeed a great year! I'm reminded by those who visit Maplewood High School of my basketball picture remaining on the wall. I truly left my mark as a player and look back at that time with a fond smile. It was like I finally found the light that led me out of the monstrous quicksand drowning me. I could breathe again.

I was excited about the scholarship, but something kept me from taking this huge step. I was afraid to travel too far away. I had never been to another city except attending Murfreesboro for basketball camp. Back then, it seemed like a 2-hour ride as opposed to a 45-minute ride. It scared me beyond belief to be so far away from the only place I had known to call home. My entire childhood was in this town. The loving community that raised me was in this town. All the experiences that made me who I am were nestled in each nook and cranny of this beautiful place. Most of all, my Mama was in this town.

As my senior year ended, the time had come to prepare for college. I thought about how my mother could only study till eighth grade, and I began to fear leaving Nashville. I was terrified of going far from everything I had ever known. As decisions were being made and I had to go to different states to visit colleges, I had yet to learn the best college. All the visits to faraway cities and huge campuses left me overwhelmed. So, I did what most inner-city kids do. I decided to stay close to home and entered a volunteer state community college headed for a nursing degree. That's what my Mama wanted me to be. I lived for my Mama in a variety of ways for many years. I believed that whatever your Mama wanted for you was what you had to do, especially since I was Mama's baby girl. Her goal was for me to be a nurse, and she hoped I would have a husband that would have a successful career as well.

So, I let my love and trust in my Mama decide where I would go for college. Her dreams became mine, and I fashioned my life to make her happy.

For me, if Mama was content, I was content.

~Chapter 9~

'The Unexpected Pregnancy'

Starting college can be intimidating, especially when
you're among the first people in your family to do so.
It takes much strength to go down a road nobody has
traveled. What beasts would you encounter? What
monsters would crawl out of their dark spaces and stand
in your way like horrific barricades? Would it stop you
from going through with it? Or would you make your way
past it? Fight until you're bloody and bruised to emerge
victorious on the other side.

I had yet to determine which one of these scenarios
would be my outcome. All I knew was that this was what
my Mama wanted. I was pressured to break a years-long
cycle that governed the women in my family. Mama only
studied till the eighth grade, and most people started
working rather than focusing on finishing their education. I
was deviating from the norm, but it was a deviation that
made my community proud—especially my Mama.

Mama saw something in me. She lived vicariously through my achievements. I was going to be the prodigy—the success. And I only wanted to be what Mama desired. I lived for her, after all. I wanted to become a woman that would make my Mama proud, and going to college was the first step. The fact that I picked a state college close to home was a huge source of comfort. Anytime I felt homesick or alone, I could take a 45-minute drive back to my hometown and spend the night in my childhood home. I was attached to my hometown, and leaving it behind, even for a nearby college, was difficult.

Once I started in a Volunteer State College, I was alone. For the first time in my life, I wasn't surrounded by the love and support of my community. It made me realize how blessed I was to have such support back home. Because college showed me how lonely life could be. It could feel bleak and quite dark. I was happy I was getting my education, but it was different from attending high school back home. When I ran into a problem, I had to deal with it by myself. I couldn't go whining to my Mama or wait for someone else to solve it. As I was away from

surveillance and supervision, I fell into some dark things—
bad habits.

And studying was a lot more complicated than I had
imagined. I had focused so much of my energy on
basketball throughout middle and high school, and now I
was underprepared for a nursing degree. My Mama
wanted me to go ahead with this path, so I agreed, but
going through with it, studying for exams, and sitting
through long classes seemed like I had bitten off more
than I could chew. It wasn't like I was performing poorly
academically, but it was still a huge culture shock.
But I powered through because becoming a nurse was
Mama's dream, so I made it my dream.

I finished the first year with good grades and a
motivated attitude. I had found a balance at college and
clung to it to get through my nursing degree. But then
something happened that would change the trajectory of
my life in a way that I could've never imagined. It was so
suddenly out of the blue. It was like a sneaky miracle of
God. At least, that's how I saw it at the time. I was caught
off guard. It landed in my lap without my knowledge.

While on summer break after my first semester, I met a dreamy man who swept me off my feet with his smooth words. I was young and impressionable, so I fell for his charm. He was five years older than me, and I was tempted to take steps that weren't benefiting me or my future. I was young and falling for an older man who gave me all his attention. He would say these sweet things that clouded my mind and judgment. I started falling for him. I had known him for a while because he had pursued me since I was 16. He would always say, *"Hey, Trina,"* with that certain sparkle in his eye. And those eyes were my downfall.

A simple greeting would have me giggling from the ticklish butterflies surrounding my stomach.
I was swooning. I remember as I got older, he would always say, *"When you turn 18, I 'm going to marry you."* I could only respond with a sheepish smile. My words would catch in my throat, and my heart would beat so hard I'd feel it in my ears. I was an emotional mess.

With his words, he made a place for himself in my heart. A place that I gave so much love to. So, when I

83

turned 18 and returned home for semester break, we went on our first date. He took me to a motorcycle meet on Jefferson Street in Nashville. I still remember what I ate that night. A fish sandwich and an orange crush drink. A combination I adore to this day. It was a magical night. I had not been on a proper date with a man I liked. And he liked me so much. I felt like I was flying throughout the night. My feet wouldn't touch the ground. I recall sparkling lights, his intoxicating eyes, my flirty giggles, and his arm around my shoulder. I felt like I was on top of the world. He made me feel beautiful.

All those years of putting him off and the wait was worth it for that one night. I was still young, so it didn't take much to impress me. I was just happy to have his company on a beautiful night. And that's all it took. From that point, we were in a relationship.

After returning to college for my second year, you can imagine my hesitation to return now that I have this man in my life! But I went back for an entire semester. I was dedicated to fulfilling Mama's dream and building my future. After my third semester, it was time to start practicing. All the information that I acquired over the last year had to be implemented in the practical realm. I was so close to putting all the information in my head to good use.

But it seemed that fate had other plans for me. It was like the rug got snatched from under my feet, and I lost my balance, tumbling to the ground. All of my plans for the future were in vain. The blank canvas I thought I could paint with my colors was stained in the blink of an eye. And I had to follow the color pattern set for me. I found out that I was pregnant.

This was my first pregnancy. My first child. My beautiful daughter Kenishea. It was a strange feeling. My first instinct was fear. I was terrified. Shook to the core. I had no plans of becoming a mother, especially at a young age and in the middle of my journey to becoming a nurse. I was the youngest of my family, and I was my Mama's baby. I couldn't imagine having a kid of my own to take care of and love. I was very vulnerable when I got the news of my pregnancy. I was paralyzed with the fear of the unknown. I was still figuring stuff out about who I was as an individual. I was away from home for the first time in my life, and I felt alone. I felt lost. I knew that this would transform my life completely. Nothing would remain the same. There was no way that anyone could be prepared for something like this. It was a force of nature—something I couldn't control or change.

A mother has to be protective, caring, kind, loving, and nurturing. I was raised by one of the strongest women I have ever seen, but I didn't know if I could live up to my Mama. She was a force to be reckoned with, making it seem effortless. I could spend my whole life trying to imitate her and still fall short. I had some big shoes to fill, and I was scared to see how Mama would react when she found out. I knew how important it was for her that I became a nurse. I was supposed to break the cycle. I felt like I would be disappointing her. It was my overthinking and paranoia that got the best of me. I was so scared about what others would think that I pushed away my happiness. My happiness of becoming a mother. Of course, I was worried and scared, but I was still happy. I would have a baby—my child.

I was so caught up in my thoughts that I didn't even think about how it would feel when my baby wrapped their tiny hands around my finger. I saw their first smile and words when I heard their first laugh. All those moments were etched with happiness. I might not have been able to live up to my Mama, but I still loved my daughter. She brought me joy that nothing in my life could even come close to. It was sweet and fulfilling.

"Giving birth and being born brings us into the essence of creation, where the human spirit is courageous and bold and the body, a miracle of wisdom."

– Harriette Hartigan

My gorgeous Kenishea was born on June 18th, 1984.

~Chapter 10~

'Releasing The Beast of Addiction'

Rose-tinted glass.
So delicate.
It could shatter with a slight touch.
The tip of my finger would suffice.
I stare in horror as it all comes crumbling down.
And a deadly monster waits on the other side.
Towering over me as I look up with trembling hands.
It was so easy to slip.
And now, I was paralyzed.

***

After the birth of my daughter, things were good for a while. I was so in love. I was wrapped up in the man who made me feel like the most beautiful girl in the world. He was the father of my child, and I introduced him to my family. We had to stay at my Mama's house until we could support ourselves. And I needed all the help I could get with the baby.

I adored my daughter but didn't know how to be a mom.

I was so caught up looking after my daughter that I missed all the signs. I was looking at the man who slept in my bed through rose-tinted glass. Everything was washed with a golden hue of love and infatuation.

I could never imagine him as someone other than the loving man I thought he was. I was caught in the motions of being a new mom and having a man in my life. I enjoyed the companionship—the comfort. I didn't have to sleep through lonely nights. Instead, I had warm arms wrapped around me, feeding me more lies and delusions.
He blinded me, but my family could see it all. All the red flags. Especially my brothers. It's because they knew me well and adored me. They just wanted the best for me, Kenishea's father, wasn't it.

I ignored it for the longest time. At first, I didn't notice anything apart from the ordinary. But soon, it all unraveled. Slowly, everything fell apart, and I was left in the shambles of my life.

I began to notice that my brothers were angry a lot, especially the one who was closest to me. It started with general disdain, but then it became violent. I swept everything under the rug until I couldn't heed it anymore. My brother and my daughter's father started to fight physically, and, at one point, the situation escalated so much that they began a shootout.

After the shootout, it wasn't feasible for this man to spend the night at our home anymore, so I had to move away from my mom much earlier than I had intended. It was like the anxiety I felt while deciding which college to go to all over again. Being away from my Mama was the worst experience, and I wasn't ready to live independently.

Especially with Kenishea. I was a young mother and had no idea what I was doing. I was snatched away from my family at a time when I needed the most familial support. I felt stranded. Lost. I was also a little angry at my brothers. Why didn't they like the man I was sharing my life with? Did they not want me to be happy? I got my answers soon enough. I realized how blind I had been.

After we were forced to go out and get our College Hill Apartments apartment set on the TSU campus, I became more informed about why my family was so angry and hostile with Kenishea's father. My family began telling me some stories about the guy I thought I loved, but I was too far into it to believe them or research what my family told me about him.

I didn't want to see it, even if it was true. I had found love for the first time in my life. I had a baby with him. I couldn't believe all the horrible things I was hearing. The worst part was that he hid it all from me. It wouldn't have hurt so much if he had been honest and transparent about his life. I didn't want my rose-colored fantasy to end so soon. But I had to face the reality. My family was telling the truth. They told me that he had been in jail for robbery and was a junkie who used drugs. My first reaction was utter disbelief. How could I not have seen it? I lived with the man and didn't realize he was using drugs! Maybe I didn't want to see it.

My family thought that the more dirt they shared about him, the more I would want to leave him. But they were disappointed that it only encouraged me to stay longer. I don't know why. I should've taken my daughter and run for the hills at the first red flag. And I didn't want my baby growing up around drugs and illegal activity. But for some unexplainable reason, I stayed. I still loved him.

As I stayed a little longer, I started to see things that showed me that what my family had said about him was true. But even with the evidence, I still did not want to believe what my family said about him.

I would do anything to believe my delusions. I remember one time when I was taking my daughter Kenishea to the doctor for a checkup. I opened the car door, and a bottle fell out and broke in the street where we were parked. I knew he was known for keeping a clean car and had a small broom and dustpan in the trunk.

So, I opened the trunk, reached to grab the broom and dustpan, and caught a glimpse of a brown bag. My curiosity got the best of me, and I opened it. The sight only confused me further. I was looking at a spoon, some cotton, and needles. I almost did a double take. It was like the world around me stopped for a moment. Everything was still, and I was caught in a terrible time loop.

My family's words echoed in my head in a sinister tone. My ears were ringing, and I could feel my heart beating in my throat. My mouth fell open for a minute, and reality set in. I was racking my brain for any explanation that would prove my family wrong. I made myself believe that somebody had stashed something in his car, and he did not know about it or that he knew a doctor.

So, while he was at work, I called my Mama and explained to her what I had found, and she said, *"That's what your brothers have been telling you all this time, Trina."* So, I went to his workplace and took some lunch with me to have an excuse to initiate a conversation. I confronted him about what I had seen in the trunk of his car. I said it all. The spoon. The cotton. The needles. I pressed him for an explanation. I needed him to say something. Anything that would prove my brothers wrong.

Like most of us addicts who are stuck in the first stage of our addiction, he found himself in denial. And that was his story. He said he had been holding it for a friend who didn't want his wife to know. He swore it was not his and did not have time for that life.

Wanting to keep up my deluded denial of what kind of a man he was, I again believed him. And from that moment onwards, I thought of him every single time. Every lie. Every excuse. I fed into his denial because I was in denial myself. I didn't want it to be true, so I took his lies in jest.

One day, when I came home, and he was gathered in the kitchen with his nephew and a friend with the door shut, I knew his glass castle of lies was about to crumble to dust.

I walked in and asked, *"What are you doing?"* I expected more lies. More excuses. But for the first time, he said it like it was. He said it plain and straight, *"We're getting high."* I didn't know how to react to the truth. I had been waiting for the ball to drop. And it finally did. I didn't know what to do with myself. Of course, I was angry at first. I was fuming. All of his lies played themselves on repeat in my head.

Everything my family had been telling me was finally out in the open. They had been right all along. And I had been a fool. But the anger dissipated into something else.

Something strangely familiar. I was shocked by the words that came out of my mouth. I turned around and said, ***"Well, I want some."*** I remember the whole time arguing with him and having my 3-month-old baby Kenishea in my arms. His first reaction was, *"NO! You don't ever want to do this!"* I said, *"If you can do it and love me, I can too."* His nephew went on to say, *"She can do it in a cigarette. But, Trina, you should never do it with a needle."* The conversation felt like a dream—a surreal moment. I couldn't believe I was doing all this with my baby in my arms. I was thinking about doing drugs while holding my Kenishea to my chest.

The best gift he ever gave me was never to use IV drugs. He said that instead of injecting the drug, he put it in a cigarette. So, to keep me quiet, my baby daddy and his nephew rolled me up two or three cigarettes with cocaine, and I began to feel a part of a sense of love and belonging. It was a tragic end to this whole fiasco. I got sucked into it. My first couple of times using cocaine, I did not get the effect I had expected, so they told me I was smoking too fast and wasting it, and it cost too much. It's funny how wasting the cocaine was their biggest worry.

So, then they showed me how to snort it. It only took the next time that he did not come home that I figured out that he was out partying without me, so I took it upon myself to go to the cut where he walked the trail to cop his dope, and I knew from prior conversations that he got it from a guy called Birdsong. After seeing Bird, I approached him and said, *"Rob sent me to get a 40-piece."*

All I was greeted with was pure anger. His face was ballooned and red, and I could almost make a snarl out of his mouth. He said, *"He knows better than to send you over here doing this. Tell him I said he needs to come to get it."*

I said, *"He's at work, and his friend is at the house waiting on me."* There was no friend whatsoever. So, he began to serve me, and if you know anything about addiction, then you would know that I was off to the races, and any extra money that came about was accounted for with the dope man.

Growing up, I always remembered the old saying, *"The first one is always free. "* My sister gave me my first joint. The father of my child gave me my first taste of cocaine, and his nephew showed me how to use the pipe. I guess this is how we get confused about what love is. We confuse toxic dependency and a fleeting high as this idea of love. That wasn't love. That was an addiction. And it trapped me in his sharp claws, sinking me in further. And getting out had its price.

After finding my way to cop my own, I usually kept a job and only used it on the weekends. That was until I started attending the club and noticed you could buy it, too. Once, while we were hanging out at the club, Rob had a bright idea. He said, *"Let's make us some money, so we never have to worry about running out of cocaine."* And so, that's what we did.

Another dark road beckoned us. But it didn't end how we expected it to. It resulted in us breaking up several times, going to jail, being evicted from place to place, and leaving my kid with my Mama.

It still haunts me to this day. My Mama didn't deserve that. She had cancer, and her junkie daughter's children were the last thing she should've been worrying about. But my Mama wasn't my priority at the time. Neither were my kids. All I thought about was drugs.

 It didn't matter that she had cancer. It was the drugs that were more important. To me, it was not that I did not love her. It was just that I could not stop the need to want more.

~Chapter 11~

'The Vicious Cycle'

My mind separated from my body.

I lost all control.

It wasn't even me anymore.

I didn't recognize myself when I looked in the mirror.

Where did that young girl with hopes and dreams go?

Was she still stuck underneath the sunken eyes and

quivering lips?

Or had I lost her?

What had I become?

***

Everyone around me had high hopes for my future.

My Mama, my siblings, and my community.

They all saw me as this bright girl destined to go far in life.

I was good in school, had a job at a very young age, was

good at sports, and went to college. They saw me as the

girl who would do it all—a success story.

But fate's cruel hand painted all their hopes and mine with

the darkest shade of black. I had more of a role to play in

that massacre. I'm not blameless.

You see, even my neighbors had high hopes of me achieving the highest level, which would only be a college level at the time because the WNBA (Women's National Basketball Association) was unavailable. I truly saw myself as a talented basketball player, traveling the world, winning trophies, and making my mama proud.

And when I started nursing school, I saw myself becoming a practicing nurse, helping those in need. It wasn't like I abandoned all my hopes and dreams in the blink of an eye. It happened gradually. Sneakily. I was so blindsided by the constant high influencing my brain that I didn't even realize that my dreams were slipping through my fingers.

I had become a shell of the bright young girl I once was. I couldn't even recognize myself. Was I the Trina my mama doted on? Was I the Trina that my brothers adored and protected? Was I the one that Herschel wanted me to be? No. Not even close. It's effortless to blame my addiction for my actions.

Addiction is a complex and multifaceted monstrosity that can hurt anyone. It hijacks the brain's reward system.

Drugs can cause the brain to release large amounts of dopamine, leading to intense feelings of euphoria and reinforcing drug use.

Over time, the brain becomes desensitized to the effects of dopamine, leading to the need for larger and more frequent doses of the drug to achieve the same level of pleasure.

It neurologically transforms the architecture of your brain and makes you feel like you need the drug to feel good. And every time, you desire more. Just one more hit. One more line. One more sip. And you fall down the dark hole of addiction.

I didn't even realize that my desire to get high could lead to negative consequences. I saw it as something fun. And escape. I didn't know then, but my addiction created problems with my relationships, work, and finances. I could barely keep a job down. I was unemployed and would spend any scraps I could gather on more drugs.

Being high always made me do risky behaviors I never thought possible. I was driving under the influence, which could've resulted in accidents, injuries, or even death.

But I didn't care. I knew there were treatments for what I was going through, but to be a part of those treatments meant I had to admit I had a problem. And that was always the thing that got me in the end. Denial. I didn't seek help until it was forced on me. In jail.

Yes. I went to jail. My charges range from possessions for resale to carrying weapons to assault. I didn't know what took over me. The terrifying part was that my family members filed the assault charges.

My deluded, drug-addled lifestyle had consumed me so much that I was losing the one thing that constantly supported me. My family. The people who raised me. The people that I would do anything for. My Mama. My brothers. I had become a stranger to them.

I was fighting, shooting, and damaging my family's property. I was a monster. And they were so angry at what I had become that they fought back. I didn't blame them. It's hard to see a loved one throw their life away in the name of drugs.

By the time WNBA was created, my dream, I was serving time for my last sentence in 1996 and released on

April 27, 1997. And it all started with that damn rolled-up cigarette filled with cocaine. Getting arrested can be a terrifying and life-changing experience. Suddenly, everything you once knew has been upended, and you find yourself at the mercy of the legal system.

I ended up at the sheriff's department's detention center. I was in a space of loneliness, despair, and isolation for the first 48 to 72 hours. But it felt familiar when I watched the circus of events unfolding before me. The people with the same behavior as me were confined in one compound, and the characteristics I portrayed on the streets were the same as those displayed inside the system.

Some of those behaviors were relationships with the inmates or the staff in the facility. Others included contraband and things considered contraband, whether clothing, shoes, jewelry, cigarettes, or candy not sold on the regular commissary toothbrushes.
You name it. Outlawed objects appeared at your fingertips. Most items were brought in by clients throwing them over the fence. People did whatever they could to

get by in prison. They didn't have any family or friends waiting for them. They were on their own, so survival was a priority. People who end up in prison don't have much in the name of family, which is usually how they end up there. I used to be one of the lucky ones.

My entire life, until I was incarcerated, my family was beside me, supporting me. I had their protection and love surround me, and I felt unstoppable. But then I went to jail.

After my repeated offenses, my Mama passed. Perhaps she couldn't bear it anymore. And it felt like someone had gutted me. My lifeline was gone. Who would I depend on now?

Before my addiction, I was my mother's right hand, intimately familiar with our family's affairs and her matters. My active involvement and support marked this pre-addiction period, starkly contrasting the challenging times that would soon follow.

During the phase when my mother struggled with colon cancer, I was ensnared by the clutches of addiction. This dire situation robbed me of the capacity to be the daughter my mother needed during her battle with illness. Instead of being her pillar of strength, I was mired in the depths of addiction's grip, unable to offer the comfort and care a loving daughter should provide. The heartbreaking reality was that my addiction held me captive, preventing me from being there for my mother during her most vulnerable moments.

In the aftermath of her passing, a profound weight settled upon me – a weight I could not confront or comprehend fully. The very substances that held me captive also hindered my ability to grieve. Instead of processing the loss of my mother, I resorted to using drugs to avoid the emotional turmoil that her absence brought. This toxic cycle was fueled by the desperate need to escape the piercing pain of her departure.

It took some time, but I realized I was a part of the problem. While in prison, I participated in the widespread culture of contraband. Looking back, I didn't feel proud of what I did, but I understood the root of my behavior and the survival mechanisms that provoked me to sell cigarettes to get the things I needed and be a part of the community around me. It was customary for most incarcerated people to have some form of support outside of the facility. Some received care packages on Christmas; I didn't even have that.

It wasn't like I had no family. I had several familial relations outside of prison who were alive and well. I learned a lot during my time in prison. While behaviors and restoration processes are in place within the prison system, it takes a while before an individual truly morphs their nature. It took me two tries in the same treatment program for that magical moment to happen, but the biggest shock was that I had support as I walked out the door and went straight into a reentry program where other women like me supported me throughout my stay. I believe in long-term recovery and a very extensive support system.

Jail can be a wake-up call, a chance to reflect on your choices and the path you've been on. It can catalyze change, a moment to reevaluate your priorities and commit to a better future. Perhaps it was what I needed at the time to seek help for my addiction. I never thought getting arrested could be an opportunity to build new relationships and find support in unexpected places. Because in jail, I realized that I needed help. I saw the women around me and knew I didn't belong there.

I remember going to jail back in 1995 and doing an 18-month sentence. I was in block "C." Prisons have programs for addicts, and many of the women in my block were a part of that program. They went to meetings and took part in the treatment plan. At first, I saw it as a scam. I would be across from the women who were in treatment, and I would mess with them, saying things like, *"Man, y'all like getting brainwashed." "Ya'll know you will do the same thing when you get out."* I saw them as the enemy because deep down, I knew that I needed the help that they were getting. But then, I was still in denial. Perhaps I accepted the fact that I was an addict. But I still didn't want help. I thought it was unnecessary. I believed that I was past the point of help. Nothing could make me want to stop using.

So, I projected my negative thought patterns onto the women trying to improve.

Most of them would try and speak, but they were not allowed to speak to those in the population or those not in treatment. I would even go so far as to call them, *"Treatment hoes."* It was disgraceful. But I soon realized what I was doing. I took a good, hard look in the mirror and tried to find familiar lines to trace across my cheeks. But I couldn't find any. I was not the Trina that my mama had raised. I didn't like the person who was staring back at me.

It was 1996 when my spirit was awakened as I gathered with 101 other women in a pod to determine if this was the life that was forecasted for me or if there was a better route.

-

~Chapter 12~

'The Counselor Who Cared'

I was drowning in a mess I created with my own hands. I sank into a pit that I dug with my actions. I believed that I was above getting help. It's funny how we ridicule people who are different from us. Sometimes they're better than us.

My dislike for the women in the program stemmed from a deep-rooted feeling of envy. They were taking the steps I was too scared to even think about. It was easy for me to stay in a bubble of denial and point fingers at the ones doing the work. As I mentioned before, the effects of prison are not immediate. I didn't accept the fact that I needed help until I was serving my second sentence. It took me that long to absorb the idea of me having a problem.

I was my biggest enemy. A monster in disguise, making me unrecognizable to myself. I had lost who I was. I used to be so sure of myself. I knew what I wanted to be and how I would get there.

But as I sat behind bars and counted my days to freedom, something broke in me. And it remained broken for years until I decided I was broken, but I also had the tools to fix it. I just needed to stop kidding and join the women in the same position. The only difference was that they knew they could be better.

This epiphany didn't reach the doorstep of my mind on its own. It was the grace of someone steadfast and unique that I finally took a step toward recovery. You see, some people that we encounter have a special role in our lives. We cross paths with them because they are meant to better us in one way or another. You can see them as your guardian angels.

Some people's presence in your life can be a source of strength, trust, development, and recovery. Such was a person that I had the pleasure of encountering within the guarded walls of a women's prison. I admit it's a strange place to meet someone who could change the trajectory of your life, but my life wasn't exactly consistent.

So, it seemed fitting that I would find my guardian angel in prison. And the person in question was the director of treatment. The same woman whose program I used to make fun of and look down on. The same woman I believed to be wasting the other inmates' time and dragging them into an unnecessary process. The same woman who I thought would never be able to crack me. One fateful day, she approached me and said, *"It's one thing you are afraid to get help, but do not stop those who want help."*

I replied, *"I'm not scared to get help; I just know it doesn't work."* She then began to say, *"I'll tell you what; let's make a deal. If you come to treatment for 30 days, I promise you that I will ensure you have a bottom bunk for the rest of your time here in jail."*

Having a bottom bunk in prison was like having a gold mine, especially for someone like me who came to jail smaller than a telephone pole and left weighing over **400 pounds**.

It was an exciting offer, but I still took my time with it. I waited a while before answering, and she always came by to ask, *"Have you made up your mind, chicken shit?"*

She was very blunt, and I think that's what intrigued me about her. So, after multiple days of her asking me, I said, *"Yes, I'll be ready on Monday."* All she had to say about my decision was, *"Good. Make sure you say all your goodbyes and sell all your cigarettes because you cannot bring all that behavior over here."* I couldn't help but let out a little nervous laugh when I said, *"What are you talking about?"* She just rolled her eyes, looking past my bullshit, *"Everybody knows what you do in here."* I confidently retorted, *"You can search me now, and you won't find anything."* "I know because you have all your runners doing it for you. Don't worry. We're going to work with you to help you change all those negative behaviors," she explained sternly.

It seemed I couldn't slither past this woman. She had eyes like a hawk, and I felt she could read me like an open book. I couldn't hide behind my lies and excuses anymore. However, she was wrong about a tiny thing. Little did she know, the guards would pick up money from people who owed me, and I paid them anything between $50.00 to $100.00 to bring me a pack of cigarettes.

I sold a pack for $40.00 and a single cigarette for $5.00. I let them get a roll-up if they could not afford a $5.00 cigarette. A roll-up is a tobacco rolled up in a tissue-like wrapping paper, which costs you **$3.00**. This was my only survival because I did not have any family support.

One of my fondest memories is that I always ensured that everybody ate, and nobody went hungry. I would find the people who didn't have anything and stocked all my *'zoo zoo's and wam wam's'* in their drawers.

It was good that I started going to treatment because the warden had come to me and posed a threat, *"Frierson, I know you're the supplier for cigarettes, and if anybody else other than a family member puts any money on your books, I will freeze your account and put you in segregation!"* I looked her straight in the eyes and walked away.

So, I began giving away all my goods, only leaving enough to last me 30 days in treatment. Initially, I intended to do the 30 days, get a bottom bunk, do my time, and get out. After I was moved over to treatment, Ms. Marlow came to me and said, *"Trina, you're a brilliant girl, and you have children that need to be taken care of. I want to see you make it because these people do not think you can make it in life and that you will spend the rest of your life inside these walls.* I scrunched up my nose at her words and said, *"Not me."* She looked me up and down with a strange look as she spoke, *"Prove it then. Stop selling cigarettes and stop going with three or four different people. Make a change for yourself."*

I remember Judges coming into the program and her making me tell my story in front of everyone. They would commend me for trying to make a change. I even remember Thomas Hollywood coming out and doing a film on doing the right thing when nobody is looking. I was able to be a part of that film.

As things began progressing in the treatment program, I struggled to get up for group meetings at 6 a.m. One of the main reasons was that they had me on meds like Thorazine, Trazadone, and Litamine which made me sleepy and drowsy. It was believed that this would keep me from acting out. Plus, I was not used to structure.

Other women in the group made my bed and did my laundry. This was good until someone called me out on my old behavior. I still remember what they said, *"The only thing that was missing was the dope. You're acting like you're still dealing on the street."* And the truth in their words struck me like a punch in the gut. Having people doing everything for me and having multiple relationships was just a manifestation of the toxic patterns I developed outside prison. They called me out on my behavior, and the counselor in the group decided to have a one-on-one with me to confront my self-destructive pattern.

Some of her first questions were about my childhood and how I grew up, after explaining that I grew up in a somewhat decent home where my mother was responsible for raising six kids. I had somewhat of a breakthrough moment when I recalled what my mother always said to me, *"You didn't get bad until you got grown."* I can attest to that. My last charge was a wake-up call for me. It was April 26, 1996.

I think my biggest strength during my time in prison was my daughter. I had decided that even if I didn't want to improve for myself, I needed to improve for her. She wasn't born an addict but lived that life with me. She was on my arm when I was dealing with the streets. I knew she deserved a better mother. I was released on April 27, 1997, and I spent time reflecting on my life. All I was left with was guilt and regret for what I had done.

~Chapter 13~

'My Penalties, My Blessings'

Family is a wondrous human connection that embodies unconditional love, unwavering support, and an unbreakable bond. You are forever linked by blood or choice, sharing the ups and downs of life, and helping each other navigate through any challenges that come your way whether you're gathering around the dinner table, taking a road trip, or spending quality time together. Therefore, no one can ever underestimate the warmth and comfort of the family.

Your familial relationships encompass the people who know your quirks and idiosyncrasies, your strengths, and weaknesses, and they embrace you for who you are. Familial bonds are so intricately woven into our existence that they always find their way back to us no matter where we are or what we do. I grew up in a tight-knit community, and I know the feeling of having unwavering support around you all the time. I was raised with much love and kindness, and these bonds transcended those of blood. I knew the importance of my chosen family. But there is one relationship that you can't quite pick—the relationship between a mother and a child.

Motherhood is a profound and life-changing experience filled with a rollercoaster of emotions. It's a journey of self-discovery, sacrifice, and unconditional love that forever alters a woman's life. From the moment a mother lays eyes on her child, an unbreakable bond is formed that transcends time and space. It's a deep connection, a love that knows no boundaries, and an unparalleled sense of purpose.

Motherhood is an emotional rollercoaster filled with moments of immense joy, pride, frustration, worry, and self-doubt. It's a constant battle between wanting to protect your child from the harsh realities of the world and wanting to teach them how to learn and grow on their own. But through it all, a mother's love never wavers, and she will always be there to pick up the pieces, wipe away the tears, and offer a listening ear. Motherhood is truly a journey like no other, one that is filled with an abundance of love, laughter, and tears.

And one that is worth every single moment. My relationship with my mother was that of immense love. I lived for my Mama. She was the strongest woman I ever knew, and I always wanted to be like her. But, when the time came for me to become a mother, fate had different plans. I did become a mother, but I lost many years of motherhood to my addiction. And I regret that every day. Looking back on my experience as a mother, I am overwhelmed by a heavy feeling of regret in my chest that consumes me in ways I never imagined. It feels like remorse, sadness, and disappointment that stem from the choices that I've made. This regret weighs heavily on my heart and mind. I see it as a painful realization that I can never go back in time to make amends or amend the mistakes that I have made. I might've had children like my mother, but I don't believe I lived up to her.

As a young girl, I remember not wanting to play with girly toys, but I accepted them because my mother bought them. But I always played with my brother's toys when she was not around. As I grew old, I played basketball and football with the boys. I asked for a boy's bicycle, masculine overalls, and Levi jeans for men. I even remember playing house and wanting to be the father. I do not know where these strange thoughts and feelings about hypermasculinity originated, but they were dominant during my formative years.

I would've fulfilled these tendencies long ago if it were up to me. But my mother had different plans for me, and I ended up having three beautiful children. Out of the three of my children, I was sober only for my first child. My first child, my daughter Kenishea, was healthy and was born on or a day before Father's Day. She was the second grandchild of my mother, as my oldest brother had a son by then. My first daughter was not born to an addict, but she experienced it all with me. She might've been born to a sober mother but didn't grow up with one.

I remember some of the poems that she wrote. They contained things that no child should be writing about. Kenishea vented about the accidents and shootouts that she experienced because of me. One night, I woke up to find that my daughter had taken some of my drug money and gone to the store to buy food for her and her sister.

Kenishea had to grow up too soon once her siblings were born because I was absent as a mother. She became the mother to her little sister and brother. It was unfair for her to skip her childhood like that. She didn't experience the carefree nativity of what being a child feels like. She had to be the adult because I was never around to let her be carefree. And it became worse when I had my second child because now, Kenishea not only had to take care of herself, she would also take on the responsibilities of taking care of her younger sister and brother.

Before my second child was born, I experienced a left tubal pregnancy and had the bright idea that I would never have children again. I was proven wrong by another pregnancy that struck me after Kenishea. My second child was born from addiction. My body had deteriorated because of all the drugs I had been consuming. And that took a toll on my baby as well.

Reflecting on my life journey, I recognize that my addiction significantly impacted my ability to perform well at various jobs over the years. I held a position in the cafeteria at St. Thomas Hospital, which was initially a good fit. However, as my compulsion took hold, I struggled to maintain consistency and was let go.

This trend continued as I cycled between jobs, unable to escape the grip of addiction. A major turning point occurred when my daughter Kawana was born in October 1989 with a congenital heart defect. The stress of her medical needs triggered my addiction to spiral out of control. I took time off work to support her, especially during surgeries. By her first open heart surgery at age five days, I remained sober. However, as pressures mounted, I relapsed, seeking drugs to escape.

When she required another open-heart surgery at age 2, I left her at the hospital, lying that I was going home. Instead, I went to use drugs and missed signing her consent paperwork. Thankfully, my mother intervened but gave me an ultimatum to shape up or sign over custody. After my daughter's return home, I attempted to balance caring for her and working at the hospital. A close friend, Vicki Nunn, encouraged me to contact my manager about getting treatment. Surprisingly, they were supportive and helped me enter a 30-day rehab program.

I tried attending support meetings initially but got involved with the wrong people and relapsed. Vicki never judged me, instead distracting me with social activities. I learned she supported herself through shoplifting with her sister. I unsuccessfully tried it once but got arrested on my second attempt. The consequences taught me that stealing wasn't who I was, considering I could have paid for the items. However, I prioritized drugs.

I later worked as a flag lady but showed up high, nearly causing accidents. Drivers grew angry. My addiction was endangering others. During winter, I went to work ill, unaware I had strep throat. It escalated, requiring ICU hospitalization, exacerbated by smoking crack cocaine. My mother cared for my kids while battling cancer. Only Vicki visited me, providing vital support.

After recovering, I couldn't return to the flagging job, ridden with shame and guilt. I tried warehouse work but relapsed quickly, proving my addiction had complete control. A destructive cycle of selling drugs and incarceration followed, using income to fuel addiction rather than responsibly. I was trapped, using drugs to numb the pain and escape.

One would think that my daughter undergoing multiple heart surgeries would be enough for me to stop using. But I didn't wake up from that nightmare. I miscarried twice before having my third child, and that still wasn't enough for me to get myself together.

I discovered I was pregnant with my third child Kevin when I was injured in a shoot-out. I was shot three times, twice in the leg and once in my private part. The bullet was a 22-traveling bullet, and the doctors could not remove it because it was too close to the water bag and could go either way. I could either lose my life or my baby's. Knowing I was pregnant again, just like my second child, I tried to smoke him away. I didn't want to be a mother and was doing everything to ensure it wouldn't happen again. I didn't return for any of my follow-up appointments at the clinic. My addiction was so bad that after I had my son, Kevin, I got drugs delivered to my hospital room. I remember the nurse coming in and saying, *"What is that funny smell?"* I had to take a hit so badly that I asked my brother to bring me some, and he did. That was the height of my addiction. I didn't even think of my newborn baby. Back then, I could get whatever I wanted because of my strong credit on the street. It seemed that my addiction had poisoned another one of my babies. My son did not speak for the first two years of his life. My first thought was that my poisonous soul was spreading to my children. After getting released from the hospital, I went home and stayed a day or two before returning to the streets, feeding my addiction. My kids were then left to my eldest sister, who was once a bright young lady I would always look up to. She worked at Channel Five News station. But somewhere along the lines, she developed a mental health disorder and did not feel she should be treated for it. My sister was so thoughtful that she could write and read in Hebrew. After getting clean, I tried to get her help but could not understand what the case worker was saying at the mental health co-op.

My sister, to whom I sought help, explained what the woman said. The reason I couldn't understand her words was because she was using significant terms, but my sister broke it down to me like this,

"She is saying that I do not show any signs that I am incapable of caring for myself and cannot be assessed unless I personally request it." That in itself blew me away. I could not understand, knowing that she was living in an unfit situation, and she always talked to herself. How could they deny her?

By this point in my life, my addiction had gotten so out of hand that my children were taken from me. I never thought about or worked towards becoming a good mother, but I never fathomed that my children would be snatched from me like that. They were in different homes. The oldest was sent to the girls' home in Tullahoma, the next was sent to her aunt, her father's sister, and my son was sent to Alabama to keep me from losing my rights in the city of Nashville, TN.

My counselor believed in me enough to find a place for my son. She went out of her way for me. It reached a point where so many people thought we were in a relationship because of her interest in helping me save my kids. What we had was not intimate or sexual in any way. She was stepping outside of the box of her services and going the extra mile because she saw something in me that I could not see myself. Losing my kids was the hardest thing that I had ever gone through. I knew my mother would've been very disappointed in me if she had lived to see it.

After having my third child, I did not last on the street for long. I had finished my 18-month sentence and gotten out with some tools that helped me get my life back on track, but no one would hire me, and I went back to my old stomping grounds. I got discouraged, and it only lasted two and a half months before I was arrested again. It was an emotionally taxing experience. The pain and disappointment of not achieving my goals weighed heavily on my mind and spirit. I felt like I let myself and my family down and wasn't good enough to succeed.

Recovery can be an emotionally intense journey that takes tremendous strength and courage. It can feel like a never-ending battle, with ups and downs that can be difficult to navigate. But when you find yourself on the path to recovery, it's important to remember that healing is possible. Whether recovering from physical or emotional trauma, addiction, or a mental health issue, the road to recovery can be challenging and rewarding. You may experience moments of doubt, fear, and uncertainty but also moments of hope, growth, and resilience.

It takes a lot of hard work and determination to overcome the obstacles that come with recovery, but with the proper support and mindset, you can push through and emerge stronger and more resilient on the other side than ever. It's a journey that requires patience, self-compassion, and a willingness to face your fears head-on. But as you continue to take steps forward, you'll find that the rewards of recovery are genuinely worth the effort.

~Chapter 14~

'A Home Away from Home'

From withered brown to vibrant green,
The leaves on trees make a stunning scene,
As nature turns a brand-new page,
And casts off the old, worn-out rage.
It's time to start anew, my friend,
To break the cycle and make amends,
To leave behind the hurts and pains,
And focus on what life remains.
The past is gone. It cannot be changed,
But the future is yours to arrange,
With every step you take today,
You pave the path for a brighter way.
So let your heart be light and free,
Embrace the possibilities,
Let hope and joy your spirit lift,
As you turn over this new leaf.

***

April 26th, 1996 marked a turning point in my life - a jolt that woke me up from my drug-induced slumber. I had been charged with multiple crimes - possession of cocaine, money, and weapons, one of which had a chilling body count attached. The authorities tried to pin the murder on me, but I refused to take the plea they offered me. I simply couldn't fathom accepting a murder charge, even if it meant a shorter sentence.

The debate went back and forth, and my public defender informed me I had no choice. They offered me 30 years, then 15 years, but I refused. Finally, they settled on an eight-year sentence with one year to serve and seven years on probation. The relief that flooded me was indescribable. I was so grateful that I prayed to God, promising to be a servant if He showed me that I could live without drugs.

However, the wake-up call came when I spoke to my eldest daughter in jail. I reassured her that I loved her and promised we would get a house and do better once I was out. Her response pierced my heart: *"Mama, that's what you always say when you go to jail."*

Those words hit me like a ton of bricks, and I spiraled into a deep depression that lasted for an eternity. My cellmates tried to pull me out of it, but my counselor truly snapped me out of it. She stormed into my cell, shouting my name, and telling me to stop pouting.

"TRINA FRIERSON," she bellowed, *"get your butt up and stop feeling sorry for yourself! You weren't thinking about them when you were out there!"*

And just like that, I knew what I had to do. I couldn't keep repeating the same mistakes and hurting my loved ones. It was time to be the person they deserved; the person God wanted me to be.

As I sat in my jail cell, feeling hopeless and defeated, I heard a voice call out my name. Ms. Marlow, the counselor, gave me a powerful message about taking care of myself before I could care for my children. She had come back to my facility just to talk to me. *"Trina, what are you doing here again?"* she asked me sternly. *"You know better. You have the tools to do better. It's not fair to your kids if you keep running from your responsibilities. If you don't want them, be honest and say it. But if you do, then get your act together and act like you have some damn sense,"* she said, trying to bring me to my senses. Those words hit me like a ton of bricks. I knew she was right. I had made the wrong choices, and it was time to turn things around. I couldn't keep making the system rich by getting arrested repeatedly. Eventually, I found myself standing before a judge at my sentencing hearing. He ordered me to go back to treatment and do relapse prevention. I tried telling him I had already been there and taught the course, but he cut me off. *"That might be the problem,"* he said. *"You taught it, but you didn't do it yourself."*

Those words stayed with me as I began my journey to recovery. With the help of Ms. Marlow and others who believed in me, I was able to turn my life around and become the mother my children deserved.

As I look back on my past, I realize that I was in relationships with women for survival, but one stood out from the rest. She was a friend from the streets who started doing me favors, like bringing me cigarettes from the outside world. As our friendship deepened, it turned into something more. I began to see a future with her, even though I never intended to when it all started.

But when I was finally released from prison and ready to start a new life with her, I found out that she had been sent back to prison just three months after her release. That's when I realized we didn't have a future together.

Despite this, she asked me to do her a favor and take her friend to a meeting. I agreed, not knowing that this simple favor would change my life forever. This simple encounter led me to the hallway house that became my home away from home. Keystone Recovery.

A recovery home is a haven for those who have lost their way, where they can heal their broken spirits and shattered lives. They can surround themselves with people who understand the pain and struggle of addiction—the people who will offer them unconditional love and support.

For many addicts, a recovery home is the first safe and stable environment they have experienced in years. It's a place where they can find refuge from the chaos and danger of the streets and finally begin to unravel the tangled web of trauma and addiction that has kept them trapped for so long. Keystone Recovery was the kind of place where addicts learned to take responsibility for their actions and their recovery. They were held accountable for their behavior and encouraged to overcome their addiction. I learned to live in a community, develop healthy relationships, and find a new life purpose and meaning.

The importance of a recovery home cannot be overstated. It was a place where I found hope amid despair. I found strength in the face of weakness and love during pain. For me, it was the beginning of a new life filled with joy, meaning, and purpose.

As I stepped into Keystone Recovery, I was greeted by someone whom I knew all too well, G Money. Johnnie, as she's formally known, was a part of my life when I was deep in active addiction, and she had always been there to have my back. I remembered when she gave me my first gun for free, telling me that I needed to stay protected out there because there were people out to get me. It was a gesture of kindness that I will never forget.

Now, here she was again, in a completely different setting, and this time we were both trying to recover. She was the one who taught me how to survive in the halfway house, how to make do without any food stamps, and how to find a job. She told me that I could use her bus card on her days off, and she even took me to the food bank to get some much-needed provisions.

Seeing how much she had changed since I last saw her was amazing. She had become a counselor, helping people like me to get back on their feet and stay sober. And she was still the same person who had always been there for me, through thick and thin, showing me what true friendship is all about. I was grateful for her presence and unwavering support, and I knew I could make it through this recovery process with her by my side.

She was a godsend, helping me find work and taking me to the food bank so we could both eat. And when she wasn't working as a counselor, she would even lend me her bus card so I could get around town. I knew I could rely on her. But my ex, always a thorn in my side, would still manage to worm her way into my life. She would call me using her friend Charlotte's phone time to get me to talk to her. But I knew I couldn't return to that life - Johnnie had shown me a better way, and I was determined to stick to it.

My biggest motivation to continue my recovery was my children. I wanted to become the mother that they deserved. I never wanted them to see me in a drug-addled state or stuck behind bars again.

But another thing that pushed me was how the people at Keystone Recovery, apart from Johnnie, didn't think I could succeed. There's a particular rush that comes from being underestimated or not believed. It's like a fire that ignites within you, fueling your determination to prove the naysayers wrong. For some, it's the ultimate motivation to push themselves to their limits and achieve things they never thought possible.

It can be disheartening at first when people doubt you, but if you harness that negative energy and turn it into something positive, it can be incredibly empowering. You begin to see every obstacle as an opportunity to prove yourself, and with each small victory, that fire grows stronger. It's a constant reminder that you can achieve greatness, no matter what others may think. So, the next time someone doubts you, don't be discouraged. Instead, use their skepticism as a springboard to propel yourself even further toward success.

~Chapter 15~

'My Newfound Freedom'

Reflecting on my life, I confidently say that becoming sober at 32 was my best decision. At first, sober life seemed daunting and even impossible, but I knew it was necessary for my physical and mental health.

I vividly recall the overwhelming fear and uncertainty that flooded my mind when I first contemplated sobriety. For so long, alcohol and drugs had been my crutch - my go-to solution for numbing the pain of life's challenges. The thought of giving up this familiar coping mechanism was daunting.

As I stared into the abyss of the unknown, I felt paralyzed with fear. How would I handle social situations without consuming any substance to numb my feelings, etc.? Would I still be fun and outgoing without the chemical courage that alcohol and drugs provided? Would I cope with my emotions and stressors without the drugs in my system?

But deep down, I knew my physical and mental health were at stake. I had reached a point where these substances were no longer a mere crutch but a crippling addiction slowly consuming me. And I saw that my children were at stake. If I wanted to be a part of their lives, I had to make a change. My time in jail and with other addicts opened my eyes, especially in Keystone Recovery. It was time to take control of my life and change for the better.

And so, I took the plunge and embraced sobriety with open arms. It was far from easy - the early days were filled with intense cravings and withdrawal symptoms. But with the support of my loved ones and the guidance of my support group, I found the strength to persevere.

As time passed, the fear and uncertainty slowly faded, replaced by a sense of empowerment and liberation. I no longer needed any substances to get through the day, and I could handle life's challenges with grace and resilience. Looking back on my journey, I am amazed at how much my life has transformed since I took that first step toward sobriety. It was a decision that required courage, perseverance, and a willingness to face my fears head-on. But in the end, it was all worth it - for the sake of my health, my happiness, my family, and my future.

I remember the first few months were the hardest. It was challenging to break the habit of turning to alcohol or drugs when I felt stressed or overwhelmed. But I found solace in my support group and my loved ones, who encouraged me every step of the way. They reminded me that I was not alone and could live a fulfilling life without my addictions.

As time went on, I began to notice the positive impact of sobriety on my life. I felt more present and engaged in my relationships with my family. My health improved, and I felt more energetic and motivated. I could focus more on my passions and hobbies and even started volunteering. Perhaps sobriety brought about the most significant change: newfound self-awareness and self-love. Without the substances clouding my judgment and emotions, I was able to confront the root causes of my addiction and work on healing myself from the inside out. I began to appreciate and accept myself for who I was; I was flawed.

It was not an easy journey - I had to confront harsh realities about myself and the world around me. I had to dig deep and face the pain and trauma I had been masking with substances for so long. But with each step forward, I felt a sense of liberation and empowerment I had never experienced.

As I worked through my emotions and embraced my true self, I could appreciate and accept myself in a way I never thought possible. I realized that my flaws and imperfections were not something to be ashamed of; they were integral to who I was.

With this newfound self-love came a sense of inner peace and contentment that had eluded me for years. I no longer needed to constantly seek validation from others or numb my pain with substances. I found joy and fulfillment in the present moment, cherishing the simple pleasures of life that I had previously overlooked.

Looking back on my journey toward sobriety, I am humbled and grateful for the transformative power that it has had on my life. This journey taught me to love and accept myself for who I am and my flaws. And in doing so,

I discovered a newfound sense of purpose and meaning that has enriched my life in countless ways.

I can see how becoming sober was a turning point in my life. It allowed me to break free from the cycle of addiction and start a new chapter filled with hope, love, and happiness. I am grateful for the journey and the lessons it taught me, and I am excited about the future, knowing that I am strong enough to face any challenge that comes my way.

I think that my story exemplifies redemption. After years of struggling with addiction, I experienced life on the streets, periods of homelessness, incarceration, and losing custody of my children. I received the support I needed to establish and maintain my sobriety to regain my life. Addiction had taken everything from me, leaving me with a shattered spirit and a bleak future.

But I found redemption through the love and support of those who believed in me. I received the help I needed to establish and maintain my sobriety, and slowly but surely, I began to rebuild my life.

To pay it forward, I wanted to serve women in similar situations.

As I worked towards my recovery, I couldn't help but notice the countless women going through the same struggles I had faced. Women caught in addiction and struggling to find their way out. Women who, like me, had lost everything and were struggling to regain their lives. This realization led me to embark on a new mission - to serve these women and offer them the same love and support that had helped me along my journey. I saw the need for a long-term program that addressed addiction and offered life-changing support, therapy, and job skills crucial to life-long recovery.

And so, I poured my heart and soul into creating a program to provide women with the tools they needed to overcome their addiction and rebuild their lives. It was not easy - there were countless challenges, from funding and staffing to navigating the complex world of addiction recovery. But I persevered, driven by a deep sense of purpose and a desire to give back to those who supported me along my journey.

After becoming stable in my recovery, Mending Hearts humbly began with me and my ex-partner offering help to this one woman who slept on their sofa in 2002, with community support coming in to help supply the basic necessities of food and clothing. "Looking back, I was blessed to have a cleaning service with my ex-partner, who helped financially support the non-profit for three years. We found that more and more women wanted a new way of life. The demand was more than we expected." Mending Hearts then became a 501c3 non-profit in 2004. And with more women needing change coming to their door, it was time to find a facility to accommodate them. It started with a 6-unit apartment house in a drug-infested community. "These were dilapidated, broken down old houses. I made a deal with the owner to allow me to come in and fix up the place with no money down, and after four months, I would pay them **$1,000 per month**. After the next four months, I would increase the payment to $1,500, and again, in another four months, I would pay $2,000 per month for the life of the lease with the first right of refusal. This was the business model I used over ten years to purchase 10 of the 16 properties we now own." In the early days with that first property, we had no idea what we were doing in trying to put up drywall, paint, and repair. I finally bought a 1,2,3 how-to book from Home Depot. We fixed up one unit and ran cords out the door to provide lights and water to the other five units. "It took not only me and my partner's efforts, but the ladies would also pitch in to help paint, hang doors, and clean the property. We were building community within our circle. Many magical moments happened when love and support came together to bring a bond of unity."

One by one, owners began to board up more homes in this drug-riddled community, more and more spaces were becoming available, and I was making more and more deals. But it was a struggle to stay clean in this drug-filled community. "One day, my partner and I were sitting at Charlie Bob's on Dickerson Road discussing this plight on how to get rid of the drug dealers and traffickers in the area. This was a complicated conversation because I was once a drug dealer. While in this discussion, an undercover police officer who sat behind us overheard our conversation. He offered to help us by arranging for the area to be heavily patrolled, which is what it took to drive them all out finally.

Today, Mending Hearts resides in a four-block campus, treating women for mental health and substance abuse. A peer program is offered that helps women gain employment, have educational opportunities, and work towards independence to achieve permanent housing. What sets Mending Hearts apart is that we are intentionally breaking institutional and generational curses by not penalizing people but helping them to grow to be contributing citizens in their communities. I have met others on this journey whom I would have never known otherwise. I am thankful they have believed in me and poured into helping to establish Mending Hearts to be a life-changing resource to women.

As I continued this journey, I believed that it was vital for me to go back to school and continue the education I had left behind as a direct result of becoming pregnant and the start of my addiction. Today, I hold a master's in organizational leadership. It wasn't easy working and raising kids. I'm forever grateful for my partnership with my family, who encouraged and assisted me. In its infancy, Mending Hearts owned one home and treated seven women. The program has grown to 15 homes and has served over 5,400 women, becoming a critical resource for treating women in Middle Tennessee. It was essential to me to not only help individuals but also to transform my community. The community that was there for me when I had nothing. I had to pay my respects.

Today, I am proud to say that the program is thriving. Countless women have come through our doors and left with newfound hope and purpose. They have gained the skills they need to live a sober and fulfilling life and have gone on to achieve great things - from starting their businesses to reuniting with their families.

Through this work, I have found a sense of fulfillment and purpose I never thought possible. As I watch these women transform their lives, I am reminded of the power of redemption - the power to transform even the darkest circumstances into something beautiful and life-affirming.

I wish to play an integral part in revitalizing West Nashville. I must rebuild a community where I was once a part of its demise. Mending Hearts has turned inhabitable dwellings into homes filled with hope to bring healing and beautification to my community and the women in it. One of the unique aspects of Mending Hearts is how we approach the physical space in which our program operates. The environment in which we live plays a crucial role in our overall well-being, and a room filled with beauty and warmth can be a powerful catalyst for healing and transformation.

That's why we have taken on the challenge of rehabilitating abandoned and dilapidated properties in our community, transforming them into safe and welcoming homes for the women in our program. We have turned once uninhabitable dwellings into havens of hope. But our efforts go beyond just beautification. We are committed to creating a sense of community and belonging for the women in our program, and our homes are designed to foster connection and support. Each house has shared spaces for cooking, dining, and relaxation, where our women can bond and build relationships with each other.

We have seen firsthand the impact these halfway houses have had on the women in our program. For many, it is the first time they have had a safe and stable living environment in years. It is a place where they can begin to heal from the trauma and chaos of their past and start building a foundation for a brighter future.

But not just the women in our program benefit from our efforts. By rehabilitating these properties, we are also helping to revitalize our community and make it a better place for everyone. We are giving new life to once-forgotten homes and bringing a sense of beauty and renewal to the neighborhood in which we operate.

What started as my journey toward sobriety has now become a beacon of hope for countless women. Seeing the transformation in these women's lives as they rediscover their self-worth and potential has been miraculous.

I have watched as they shed the shame and guilt that once held them back and embrace the limitless possibilities that sobriety brings. I have seen them overcome seemingly insurmountable challenges and come out stronger and more resilient on the other side.

But the most beautiful thing about this program is that it is not just about sobriety. It is about reclaiming one's life and rediscovering one's purpose. It is about embracing the power of community and connection and realizing that we are all on this journey together.

Through my work, I have found a sense of fulfillment and purpose I never thought possible. Every day, I wake up excited to see what the day will bring, knowing that I am making a difference in these women's lives.

And while I may have started this journey alone, I have since realized that I am never truly alone. I am surrounded by a community of strong, resilient women committed to supporting each other regardless of life's challenges.

In the end, my journey toward sobriety was not just about me. It was about the power of redemption and the potential for transformation within us all. It was about realizing that no matter how bleak our circumstances may seem, we always have the power to choose a different

path.

It was about discovering that we are never truly beyond

repair, no matter how broken we feel.

~Chapter 16~

'Bringing My Vision to Light'

It's mystifying to think about how we can perceive something that seems so simple and enticing, yet we delude ourselves into believing that we're exempt from the dangers. Addiction closes our eyes to the risks and convinces us that we have control when, in reality, it controls us.

But amidst the chaos and despair, there was a flicker of hope. I came to a profound realization that I had a choice, a chance to reclaim what addiction had stolen from me. With an unwavering determination, I sought help and reached out to those who understood my struggle. Through their guidance and support, I found myself at Keystone Recovery, marking a significant milestone on my journey to recovery.

Day by day, I began rebuilding; I glued back the shattered pieces of my life. I mended broken relationships, one sincere apology at a time. I reignited my passions, embracing the possibilities that lay ahead. Slowly but surely, my health improved as I nurtured my body and spiritually hydrated my mind with care and compassion. Through my recovery, I couldn't help but recognize the immense value of community. It became crystal clear that while recovering from addiction, the support of others is paramount. Addiction thrives in isolation, feasting on our shame, guilt, and loneliness. Breaking free from its grip requires more than mere willpower; it necessitates a network of individuals who can offer a haven for healing and growth.

Being surrounded by people who have walked a similar path provides a sense of belonging and understanding that is vital for recovery. In the company of those who have faced their struggles, we no longer need to explain ourselves or fear judgment. They inherently grasp the complications of addiction and provide a supportive space where we can let our guard down and be vulnerable.

Accountability is another crucial aspect of recovery, and having a community that holds you responsible for your goals can make all the difference. They offer guidance, encouragement, and gentle reminders of why you embarked on the journey to recovery in the first place. Knowing that others believe in your ability to overcome challenges and root for your success can motivate you to stay committed to sobriety.

Moreover, witnessing the journeys of those who have successfully overcome addiction can inspire hope in those still grappling with doubt or uncertainty. These individuals become beacons of possibility, proving that recovery is attainable and transformative. Their stories of rebuilding their lives, repairing relationships, and finding joy in sobriety ignite a flame of hope, reminding us that we, too, can forge a new path.

The power of community extends beyond the immediate benefits. Lifelong friendships are forged, creating a lasting support system that reinforces our commitment to sobriety and acts as a safety net during times of vulnerability. These connections become integral to our ongoing journey, providing support and encouragement.

Recognizing the significance of community in addiction recovery, I felt a deep calling to give back and make a difference in the lives of those who had walked a similar path. I understood firsthand the impact of addiction on individuals and communities, and it became my fervent belief that it was my responsibility to restore and rebuild what had been lost.

This realization led me to found **Mending Hearts** in 2004. I wanted to create more than just a rehabilitation center; I envisioned a sanctuary of healing where women could find solace, support, and the tools necessary to rewrite their stories. It was about offering more than a temporary fix; it was about empowering women to reclaim their lives and discover their true potential.

Drawing from my experiences and the information gained through my transformative journey, I meticulously crafted a program addressing every aspect of a woman's life. It was a comprehensive approach encompassing evidence-based therapies to address addiction, but it didn't stop there. I knew that true transformation went beyond overcoming addiction. It involved rebuilding self-esteem, rediscovering purpose, and equipping these women with the life skills necessary for a fulfilling future.

At Mending Hearts, we provided a treatment program and a sisterhood of support. Our community offered a safe space for women to heal, grow, and celebrate big and small milestones. Bonds were forged, stories of triumph echoed through the halls, and the flame of hope burned bright.

Our program expanded beyond the walls of our sanctuary. Women who graduated from our program became ambassadors of hope in their communities. They shared their stories, offered a helping hand to those still in addiction, and proved that recovery was possible. The impact of their collective efforts extended far and wide, inspiring others to embark on their journey of healing and transformation.

Over the years, Mending Hearts has grown exponentially. From humble beginnings with just one home and seven women, we now operate 15 houses and have served over 5,400 women in Middle Tennessee. Our program has become a critical resource for treating women, offering a comprehensive support system that extends well beyond the confines of our facility.

Every day, I am humbled and grateful for the opportunity to serve these courageous women as a guiding light on their recovery journey. Together, we are rewriting the addiction narrative, weaving a tapestry of strength, healing, and second chances. Through our collective efforts, we are building a future filled with hope, resilience, and unwavering support.

Addiction might have stolen a lot from us, but we are reclaiming our power, rewriting our stories, and creating a ripple effect of transformation that will touch the lives of countless others. It is an honor to be part of this journey, and I invite you to join us as we continue to empower individuals, rebuild communities, and prove that recovery is possible for everyone.

I wholeheartedly believe in the power of redemption and the importance of community in recovery. My addiction may have taken so much from me, but it also granted me resilience, empathy, and a deep appreciation for the beauty of a life reclaimed. Above all, my recovery has reconnected me with my mother and children and blessed me with friends I can trust on my back with my eyes closed, knowing they have my best interest as I have theirs.

As I reflect on my journey, I cannot understate the significance of my community throughout the recovery process. Community, for me, has always played a consistent and vital role in my life. Whether it was the neighborhood where I grew up or the halfway house that offered support, my community has been an anchor in times of struggle and a source of strength during the darkest days.

The role of the community while recovering from addiction cannot be emphasized enough. It serves as a lifeline, providing much-needed support, understanding, and connection during one of the most challenging journeys a person can undertake. Addiction often thrives in isolation, feeding on the feelings of shame, guilt, and loneliness that accompany the struggle. Breaking free from addiction requires more than individual willpower; it demands a network of individuals who can offer a safe space for healing and growth.

When surrounded by people who have walked a similar path, individuals in recovery feel seen and heard. They no longer have to face judgment or explain themselves because others within the community inherently understand the complexities of addiction. This understanding fosters a sense of belonging and acceptance, creating an environment where individuals can let their guard down and be vulnerable without fear of rejection.

In recovery, accountability is critical; having a community that holds you responsible for your goals can make a world of difference. Community members can offer guidance, encouragement, and gentle reminders of why you embarked on the journey to recovery in the first place. Knowing that others are rooting for your success and genuinely believing in your ability to overcome challenges can be a powerful motivator to stay committed to sobriety.

One of the most profound aspects of community addiction recovery is the power of shared experiences. Witnessing the journeys of others who have successfully overcome addiction instills a sense of possibility and ignites a flame of hope within those grappling with doubt or uncertainty. Seeing others rebuild their lives, repair relationships, and find joy in sobriety becomes a beacon of light, reminding individuals that recovery is attainable and transformative.

Within a community, individuals can exchange coping strategies, offer advice, and provide emotional support. This shared wisdom becomes a powerful resource, equipping individuals with a toolkit of strategies to navigate the challenges that may arise during their recovery journey. It's a collective effort, with everyone contributing their unique insights and experiences, creating an environment of growth and learning.

The impact of community extends far beyond the immediate benefits. Lifelong friendships were formed, creating lasting bonds that continue to provide support and encouragement beyond the initial stages of recovery. These connections become an integral part of an individual's ongoing support system, reinforcing their commitment to sobriety, and providing a safety net during times of vulnerability.

Recognizing the immense value of community, I felt a profound calling to serve women who had walked a similar path. The flames of my redemption had ignited a passion, urging me to reach out and make a difference in their lives. I realized that I knew the experience and the compassion to create a sanctuary of healing where women could find solace, support, and the tools needed to rewrite their stories.

With unwavering determination, I embarked on a mission to establish a long-term program that addressed addiction holistically. I envisioned a place where women could break free from the shackles of their negative habits and heal the wounds that had led them down this treacherous path. It wasn't just about providing rehabilitation but empowering these women to reclaim their lives, discover their inner strength, and embrace the beauty of a sober life.

Drawing from my experiences and the information I had gathered on this transformative journey; I meticulously crafted a program encompassing every facet of a woman's life. It was more than just addressing the addiction; it was about addressing the underlying issues, providing tools for personal growth, and fostering a sense of community and sisterhood.

At the heart of our program was the understanding that true transformation went beyond overcoming addiction. It involved rebuilding shattered self-esteem, rediscovering one's purpose, and equipping these women with the life skills necessary for a thriving, purposeful future. We offered evidence-based therapies to address addiction but didn't stop there. We integrated counseling, vocational training, and educational opportunities to empower these women with the tools needed to build a foundation of stability and independence.

Before embarking on the mission of Mending Hearts, my work history included both full-time and part-time positions at a printing company named Express Media. My partner and I also ran our cleaning service. Amid these professional pursuits, I vividly recall interacting with a woman named Joyce Edwards at the printing company.

She expressed a keen interest in learning more about the mission I envisioned. One memorable day, she handed me $300.00, urging me to open a checking account to kick-start the endeavor. This marked the beginning of a transformative journey that Joyce guided me through. Joyce's support didn't stop at financial contributions; she became my mentor, educating me about building a board for the mission. As we commenced housing women in 2002, it was in 2004 that we officially attained 501(c)(3) status. Joyce's unwavering dedication extended to providing a $700.00 check to facilitate filing. Her commitment went beyond monetary support; she spread the word among her neighbors and friends, garnering resources that ranged from beds and furniture to clothing. Joyce's kindness turned her garage into a makeshift storage unit for our cause. She remained a true angel, a guiding presence by my side until her passing.

Joyce's involvement was just the beginning of a more significant movement that took root in our city. The principle of a village raising a child manifested itself in philanthropy. Word spread about our mission's impact, and individuals from various walks of life contributed their resources. This collective effort translated into an influx of volunteers and service providers, significantly expanding our capacity to help those in need.

Among the motivating factors behind the inception of Mending Hearts was my former partner, Charlotte. She possessed an exceptional talent for structuring and optimizing systems, complementing my role in building resources and securing essential funding. Charlotte's dedication extended to handling a substantial portion of administrative responsibilities. But life took an unexpected turn as Charlotte chose to address her challenges stemming from past addiction, resulting in her departure from the foundation. This loss deeply affected me, as Charlotte had been a soulmate for 23 years and instrumental in building what we had once only dreamt of.

Today, Mending Hearts has blossomed into an organization that annually serves more than 400 women, including a subset of women and children. Our mission is twofold: addressing addiction and mental health to facilitate holistic recovery. We can only truly empower these women to reclaim their lives by addressing both aspects. Our beneficiaries come from diverse backgrounds, spanning nurses, lawyers, ministers, and everyday women to those in rural areas who lack the resources to break free from addiction's grasp.

The journey from its inception to its current impact has been one of community collaboration, unwavering support, and a commitment to healing and growth. As we expand our reach and help more individuals find their way to recovery, we honor the legacy of those who stood by us and helped us shape Mending Hearts into the force for good it is today.

When Mending Hearts opened its doors, the impact was profound. I witnessed the light returning to these women's eyes, their spirits rekindled by the flame of hope and possibility. We laughed, cried, and celebrated big and small milestones. Our bonds grew deeper; we became friends and sisters. The stories of triumph echoed through the halls, inspiring others to join us on this healing path. But our program's impact didn't end within the walls of our sanctuary. Women who graduated from our program became beacons of hope in their communities. They carried their stories of resilience, strength, and transformation, sharing them with others still trapped in the grip of addiction. These women became living proof that recovery was possible and that a beautiful life awaited them on the other side.

As Mending Hearts continued to grow, our community grew along with it. From our humble beginnings with just one home and a handful of women, we expanded to 15 homes and have served over 5,400 women in Middle Tennessee. We have become a trusted and critical resource for treating women struggling with addiction, providing them with the comprehensive support system they need to reclaim their lives.

Here, I have to mention Janet Warfield. She was an angel sent by God. One day, she showed up on our doorstep, expressing interest in learning more about our organization. She explained that she had a group of women who wanted to visit and hear our story. After experiencing what we do by sitting in one of our units that may not have met their initial expectations, she left feeling inspired. Following her inspiration, Janet, and her group (of women) began volunteering and organizing fundraisers to support our cause. Over time, Janet's involvement deepened, and she became a board member. From there, she utilized her accounting skills to contribute further. Throughout this journey, she became a dear and long-lasting friend. I am eternally grateful for her unwavering support not only for Mending Hearts but also for guiding me in putting my life in order financially for the betterment of my family. We are grateful to Janet and her family for their generosity and friendship.

Every day, as I witness the profound impact of our program, my heart swells with gratitude. The journey to recovery is not easy, but seeing the transformation unfold before my eyes reaffirms the power of compassion and the incredible resilience of the human spirit. It is an honor to serve these courageous women and to be a guiding light on their path to recovery.

Through Mending Hearts, we are rewriting the narrative of addiction. We are weaving a tapestry of strength, healing, and second chances. But we don't stop there. We are also committed to transforming the communities that have suffered under the weight of addiction. We strive to restore and rebuild what has been lost, to create a future where individuals can find hope, support, and the opportunity to lead fulfilling lives.

Mending Hearts is not just a program; it is a testament to the power of redemption and the resilience of the human spirit. It is a beacon of hope for those seeking recovery and a reminder that no matter how far addiction has taken us, there is always a path to redemption and a community of support waiting to embrace us.

If you are a woman in a similar predicament as I was in my earlier days, I invite you to join us on this journey of healing and transformation. Together, we can make a difference, one life at a time. Together, we can create a world where addiction no longer holds power, where individuals can rewrite their stories and embrace the beautiful lives they were meant to live. Let us support one another and build a future filled with hope, resilience, and unwavering support.

~Chapter 17~

'To Anyone Struggling—For My Strugglers'

I see a glimpse of my father lying in bed.
His eyes struggle to stay open.
Liquor bottles surround his bed in disarray.
I'm convinced I inherited his addiction.
Passed down by him in pieces.
Much like the shards of glass that drip with his liquor.

***

Life as an addict was a chaotic whirlwind, a relentless dance with darkness. Challenges lurked around every corner. Their alarming presence constantly reminded me of addiction's grip on my soul. Within the depths of my addiction, I witnessed the unraveling of my very being. The relentless pursuit of substances consumed my days, leaving me trapped in a cycle of desperation and despair. Consequences, like vengeful specters, haunted my every step. They reached far beyond the confines of my existence, casting a dark shadow over the lives of those around me.

The terrible weight of addiction bore down upon my loved ones, their hearts burdened with worry and anguish. Relationships fractured, bonds strained as the destructive force of my addiction tore through the fabric of trust and stability. Buying drugs in the streets of Nashville was like playing the lottery. It was a risky game, where you either hit the jackpot with good stuff or ended up with "wooed" —bad dope. I remember going to different people to get my fix, desperately seeking that high. But things took a turn for the worse after the devastating loss of my mother in 1993, followed by the tragic death of my brother later that same year.

The pain and emptiness I felt drove me deeper into my addiction. I went from just smoking crack to making a living out of it, thanks to the influence of my brother, BaBa. He was the one person I had a love-hate relationship with, but I would still do anything for him within reason because he's, my brother. BaBa confronted me a few months after our mother passed away, delivering some harsh but necessary truths about our new reality without her.

"You need to get yourself together because Mama is gone, and ain't nobody gonna care for you like she did," he said.

His words struck a nerve, and I made a pivotal decision at that moment. I remember splitting the next piece of crack I got in half—one section for me to smoke and the other to sell. That was the day I found the courage to enter the world of dealing drugs selling cocaine.

From that day forward, my life took a new direction. I moved from small-time deals to handling grams and then ounces. Word spread on the streets that I had a reliable customer base, and soon, people started approaching me with partnership offers.

But the partnership continued for a short time because I was already working together with my brother. The streets became a battleground for territorial control, straining our relationship further.

As my drug empire grew, so did the risks and rewards. I became the go-to person for the hottest items and even received paper food stamps as part of the deals. This went on for years, with me constantly in and out of jail. But I always had someone to bail me out and cover my back.

That is until I lost count of the days, and the missed court appearances led to arrest warrants being issued against me. My life became a vicious cycle of addiction, crime, and the ever-looming threat of imprisonment. Every day in the streets of Nashville felt like a war zone, forcing me to make perilous choices to survive.

We started playing dangerous games with our lives, like getting into cars with strangers, not knowing who they were. I remember one night when I took a guy to buy a large number of drugs, but instead, he robbed the sellers, making it seem like I was part of the setup. Luckily, the guy recognized me and didn't retaliate, but his crew did. They caught me in the projects, locked me in a room, and put a shotgun to my head while kicking me.

Amidst the terrifying scene, one person in the crowd had a moment of mercy. He said, *"Stop, man. We don't want to deal with her brothers. We'll get them another way!"*

After they released me, I went to the main man's house, and he walked me back to them, warning them never to touch me again. It seemed like the ordeal was over. Al knew I was innocent, and it was all a misunderstanding.

My next encounter with one of the ruthless gangs was in 1994 when I was still working on one of the projects. A guy named Cadillac tried to convince me to give him an ounce of weed, but I refused. In the meantime, I crossed paths with someone I had been partying with and fell asleep while he performed sexual favors on me. When I woke up, I discovered he had stolen over **$1500** and half an ounce of cocaine. Fueled by anger and desperation, I confronted him in the breezeway. When I pulled out my pistol, Cadillac emerged with a gun and started shooting. The bullets found their mark, hitting me twice in the leg and once in my private area. I drifted unconscious and awoke three days later in the hospital, only to receive the shocking news that I was six weeks pregnant. It was a painful physical and emotional awakening as I realized the consequences of the life I had been leading. I was trapped in addiction, a prisoner to drugs. They controlled my life completely.

Every day was a struggle between brief moments of happiness and deep despair. Addiction consumed me, leading to a never-ending cycle of self-destruction. "Just one more hit," I would say, hoping it would fill the emptiness.

My life spiraled into chaos. Relationships crumbled, and those I cared about lost faith in me. Sometimes, I had moments of clarity, glimpses of my old self. But the cravings quickly took over. I hit rock bottom, a dark place where hope seemed distant.

I navigated moments of struggle, loss, and excruciating pain during life's relentless challenges and ever-present hardships. However, occasional rays of hope and glimpses of redemption emerged amidst the chaos. One such ray was the enduring bond that I forged with my daughter and the grandchildren of my ex-wife, a bond that transcended the trials we faced. Together, we embarked on a journey of healing and understanding, engaging in heartfelt conversations about her mother. In those moments, I sought to offer more than just words of encouragement. I aimed to impart a profound awareness of the relentless grip of addiction and the toll it exacts upon individuals. At the ripe age of 51 and above, I reflect upon my remarkable journey, marked by triumph over adversity and the reclamation of my existence. With a heart bursting with gratitude, I proudly declare my sobriety, a steadfast companion for over 25 years. Therefore, to anyone who finds themselves locked in the relentless grip of addiction, I speak directly to you. I understand the suffocating weight upon your shoulders, the despair that gnaws at your soul. But hear me now: Help is within your reach, waiting to guide you toward an addiction-free life.

In the depths of my struggle, I discovered that I was not alone. Each day, I fought to break free from addiction. It was a tough battle, but I refused to let it define me. Support systems, resources, and compassionate individuals stood ready to extend a hand to offer solace and guidance on the arduous path to recovery. It may seem insurmountable, but I implore you to muster the courage to take that first step toward change.

In a realm beyond my grasp, I humbly express my gratitude for God's enigmatic presence. What I comprehend of this divine force is but a mere fragment of its boundless grandeur and power. I find solace in relying on this entity, my understanding of God, for it elevates me above my insignificance.

This entity led me into despair, casting me into the fiery pits of my hell. Yet, through this divine power, I could also open my eyes and perceive a path where none existed. Those who once believed I was irredeemably lost and beyond salvation were proven wrong, thanks to the grace and mercy bestowed upon me. Through these divine interventions, I rebuilt my foundation and embarked on a transformative journey alongside a circle of kindred spirits.

Within this circle of love, we embarked upon a 12-step process, a sacred pilgrimage of the soul. In their unwavering belief in me, these fellow travelers mirrored the steadfast faith of God Himself. It is through them that I witnessed tangible evidence of His omnipotence. In the spiritual realm, a belief often requires a visible manifestation. Through the love, support, and guidance of these remarkable individuals, I beheld the power of God materialize in my life. Through them, I discovered new realms of possibility, a spiritual realm where I found my place amidst a tapestry of life, love, happiness, and inner peace.

I no longer need to traverse the streets in fear, constantly glancing over my shoulder, for the night no longer holds its menacing grip on me. I rejoice at the dawn of each new day, free from the shackles of fear. I eagerly await the rising sun, no longer haunted but filled with anticipation, knowing I need not wander the nocturnal streets. The darkness, where my past traumas once thrived, is but a distant memory, for it was someone who had traversed that same devastating path, found a new way in the face of adversity, and guided me toward the light. And now, I am privileged to sit at tables with those I once thought unreachable.

These tables, you see, are graced not only by judges, lawyers, and the affluent but also by the homeless, the downtrodden, and those whose appearance and aroma may not conform to societal norms. I understand the magnitude of God's love in the presence of these diverse souls, both lost and found. Through this program, which has granted me a second chance at life, I have had the honor of encountering extraordinary individuals. Among them are the judges who dispense justice, the lawyers who advocate for truth, the millionaires and billionaires who have amassed fortunes, and those who have found themselves beneath the bridges and the radar. I am humbled to have walked alongside them, engaging in conversations transcending societal barriers.

Reflecting upon my past, I am struck with disbelief and awe. Though I know it to be accurate, it astounds me that I once sold my soul for something as trivial as the pursuit of instant gratification. Crack cocaine, marijuana, the allure of a fast-paced existence—these vices became the currency with which I bartered away my dreams. I sacrificed my soul for substances that offered no lasting rewards. I ponder why I had to endure such trials and tribulations.

Yet, with each passing day, my understanding deepens.

I firmly believe that those of us who have weathered the storms of trauma and hardship are called to stand as beacons of hope for others. We are destined to bridge the gap between disbelief and faith, for often, evidence is required to ignite the flickering flames of belief.

Our behaviors, tainted by addiction and mental anguish, often lead us to lose faith—not because God has forsaken us, but because we have forsaken Him. We struggle to trust the divine when we cannot witness its manifestation. Yet, I firmly believe that our journey through these turbulent seas of adversity, our scars, and struggles, is purpose driven. They carve a path for us to become tangible examples, guiding lights for those who will tread the treacherous terrain we once navigated.

We learn that by trusting the process, steadfastly believing, and embracing the winners' circle, God will perform miracles on our behalf, surpassing what we could ever accomplish on our own. However, it is through His people that these miracles unfold, for one cannot purchase God, peace, or freedom. Yet, we can actively participate in the process and discover a path to attain these precious gifts.

So, I am forever indebted to those who have shown me unwavering support on this arduous journey. They have become living testament of God's power, love, and grace. They embody hope, leading me to a life of abundance and boundless possibilities. Through them, I have reunited with my children, for this program instilled in me the belief that I am worthy of their love and presence.

This program has introduced me to the most extraordinary individuals, far beyond anything I could have fathomed. Around the table where the lost souls converge, I have met judges who dispense justice, lawyers who uphold truth, and millionaires and billionaires who have amassed wealth. Yet, the table is also graced by those who have found themselves without a home, toiling beneath the scorching sun, or seeking shelter beneath bridges. These souls do not conform to societal expectations; they may not bear the appearance or scent of success. Yet, they have found their place at the table in their journey from loss to redemption.

When I contemplate the insanity of my past, the depths to which I sank, I am astounded. I recall selling my soul to the allure of crack cocaine, the pursuit of an ephemeral high. My vices led me to neglect my children, family, and dreams. I abandoned my aspirations for substances that offered nothing in return. I often wonder why I had to endure such torment. But as I stand here today, I grasp a more profound truth. My struggles, my hardships, were not in vain. I firmly believe that those of us who have endured traumatic events and weathered life's harshest storms are called to stand as beacons of hope for others. We become living proof that redemption is possible, and that faith can be restored.

I believe those who yearn for salvation require visible proof, evidence of the transformative power of God's love. By sharing our stories, acknowledging our past mistakes, and embracing our flaws, we provide a roadmap for others. We emerge as tangible examples, speaking to the hearts of those who have lost their way. We become the bridge between disbelief and faith, offering a lifeline to those who stand on the precipice of self-destruction.

In my darkest moments, I have been humbled by the unwavering support of my children. They stood firm, weathering the storm of judgment and whispers as they went to school. People spoke ill of their mother, passing judgment and casting stones. But my children remained steadfast, never faltering in their love for me. They shouldered the burden of shame, their innocence tarnished by the cruelty of others. Yet, I promised myself and them that I would never keep secrets or withhold the truth. I became an open book, a testament to the power of honesty and vulnerability. I ensured they would never walk in shame because of who their mother once was. If ever they face the demons that haunted me, they would know that help is within reach, that they need not suffer in silence.

I reflect upon my oldest child, who, at the tender age of nine, stepped into the role of a mother figure. She carried the weight of responsibility, nurturing her younger siblings as best she could. In her young heart, she matured beyond her years, assuming the mantle of an adult after losing her grandmother. She remained resolute, a pillar of strength even when tossed between family members. Today, she stands tall—a robust, resilient, and entrepreneurial soul, a guiding light for her siblings.

As for my second eldest daughter, she faced trials in accepting her mother's flaws. It was challenging for her to reconcile the woman I had been to see who I aspired to become. Yet, she granted me a second chance at motherhood, a chance to rewrite the narrative. And for that, I am eternally grateful. I told her the truth about my past, exposing my vulnerabilities and insecurities. I vowed to be transparent to communicate openly about addiction and mental health, even the complexities of medication. I wanted her to understand that no topic was off-limits and that she need not bear the weight of secrecy.

Today, my children can recount their mother's journey. They can speak with conviction, dispelling the misconceptions and judgments cast upon them. They hold their heads high, aware of the path I walk and the path I continue to tread. They know that help is available and that their mother's love, though imperfect, is unwavering.

Looking back, I am overwhelmed by the resilience of the human spirit. I survived near-death experiences, the echoes of gunshots ringing in my ears, and the harrowing realization of an unexpected pregnancy. There were moments when I hovered between life and death, my consciousness fleeting. I ponder the insanity that once consumed me, my disregard for my children's well-being when I believed myself unworthy of motherhood.

In those moments, I prayed that my cocaine-infused choices would somehow spare them from a life with me. But in the end, something greater than myself saved us. It was divine intervention, restoring life not once but twice, despite my every effort to sabotage it. I hold my children close today, cherishing our restored relationships and unbreakable bonds.

And so, I continue to stoke the fires of hope for those in recovery and my family. I strive to remain open, transparent, and ever ready to discuss addiction, mental health, and the importance of seeking help. I aspire to be a guide.

During my healing process, therapy played a crucial role, enabling me to navigate the complexities of life with renewed strength. Leaving drugs behind was not an easy path. It demanded unwavering determination and resilience as I confronted the demons that had held me captive for far too long. But with each step forward, a new world unfolded before me—a world teeming with possibility and the promise of a brighter tomorrow. I reflect upon my self-destructive journey, and I can't help but marvel at the stark contrast of life since I bid farewell to the clutches of addiction. Where once there was chaos and despair, now a sense of peace and clarity permeates my days.

As my story weaves through the fabric of time, I recall one stormy night that etched itself in my memory. Rain poured relentlessly, cleansing my spirit of doubt and fear. I found solace in the company of kindred souls and fellow travelers on the road to recovery. Together, we weathered the tempest, our bond unyielding amidst the deceitful waves of addiction.

With each passing year of sobriety, I discovered a newfound reverence for life's preciousness. Each sunrise greeted me with renewed gratitude, a reminder of the infinite possibilities ahead. I beheld the world's wonders with fresh eyes, capturing the brilliance of a sunset's palette and relishing the gentle whispers of a summer breeze.

I suggest everyone embrace the perplexity of the path, for it is in the twists and turns that the true essence of growth resides. Let your sentences burst forth with the passion of your experiences, intertwining the complex and the concise, for within this symphony lies the authenticity of your story.

Let us march forward together, for the common thread of resilience binds us. And as we continue to unravel the enigma of our existence, may we inspire others with our words, actions, and unwavering belief that no struggle is insurmountable.

~Chapter 18~

'Where I Am Now'

In a world often marred by hardship and adversity, I stand tall as a luminary, an unwavering force of compassion, empowerment, and transformation. With unyielding determination, I have dedicated myself to advocating for those in recovery, incarceration, homelessness, and co-occurring disorders, painting a brighter future with every step I take.

My journey of impact and achievement has been nothing short of extraordinary. My remarkable efforts have earned me accolades and recognition from all corners, reaffirming my position as a beacon of hope in the lives of countless individuals. In 2022, I proudly stood as a finalist for the prestigious Next Awards Entrepreneur, a testament to my innovative and visionary approach to creating positive change.

The Year 2018 marked the pinnacle of my achievements, as I received the revered CEO of the Year award from TAADAS (Tennessee Association of Alcohol,

Drug Abuse, and Addiction Services). This distinguished honor exemplified my exceptional leadership skills and unwavering commitment to improving the lives of those affected by addiction and related disorders.

But my impact extends far beyond a single accolade. In 2016, I gratefully received the esteemed Humanitarian Award, a testament to my outstanding services in the field of social action. My dedication to lifting others, restoring dignity, and fostering resilience has become a guiding light, inspiring communities to come together and effect positive change.

I was humbled to be recognized as the Professional of the Year by TAADAC (Tennessee Association of Alcohol and Drug Abuse Counselors) in 2016. This acknowledgment celebrated my expertise and unwavering commitment and recognized me as a role model for fellow professionals striving to make a difference.

Embodying the spirit of transformation, I took my vision further by authoring the influential book "Exit Plan." This empowering work serves as a roadmap for individuals seeking to overcome adversity and break free from the chains of addiction. Complemented by a facilitator's guide, my book has become a source of inspiration for countless individuals and professionals alike.

My profound impact has resonated deeply within my community. My unwavering dedication to others earned me the heartfelt "Hometown Hero" title for Middle Tennessee, an honor bestowed upon me by the esteemed Darrell Waltrip Group. This recognition reflects the profound impact I have made on the lives of those around me, cementing my legacy as a true champion of compassion and resilience.

My commitment to growth and learning is evident in my achievements. I was honored with a student leadership award from Argosy University, a testament to my relentless pursuit of knowledge and personal development.

Through my unwavering advocacy, I have become a symbol of hope, igniting inspiration in the darkest corners of society. My journey is a testament to the transformative power of compassion and resilience, reminding us all that no obstacle is insurmountable and that every individual can create positive change.

My impact is not limited to accolades or titles; it lies in the lives I have touched, the hearts I have mended, and the futures I have transformed. My story is a beacon of inspiration, urging us all to embrace our innate capacity for compassion, strength, and unwavering determination. In a world that often yearns for heroes, I emerge as a guiding light, illuminating the path toward a better, more inclusive, and compassionate future for all.

In my journey through life, I found my purpose in serving others and making a lasting impact on my community. As a Community Outreach Coordinator at New Covenant Church, I had the privilege of extending a helping hand to those in need, embodying the values of compassion, empathy, and empowerment.

One of the initiatives closest to my heart was the Back-to-School drive for Tomorrow's Hope Association. I firmly believe in the power of education to transform lives and provide opportunities for a brighter future. By organizing this drive, we provided essential school supplies to children, ensuring they had the tools they needed to succeed academically.

Beyond the Back-to-School drive, I dedicated my time to helping people set up new non-profits. I understood the challenges faced by those seeking to make a positive change in their communities, and by volunteering my expertise and support, I witnessed the birth of numerous organizations that made a tangible difference in people's lives.

As a committee member for the Toy drive at New Covenant Church, I had the privilege of bringing joy and happiness to children during the holiday season. The smiles on their faces and the warmth in their hearts were constant reminders of the power of collective effort and generosity.

In my quest to create lasting change, I have taken on numerous leadership roles that allow me to contribute to the betterment of society. I serve on the Board of Directors for the Nashville Davidson County Continuum of Care Planning Council Governance. This position enables me to collaborate with like-minded individuals and work towards creating comprehensive solutions to address homelessness and related challenges in our community.

I also proudly held the position of President for TN-ARR, leading a dedicated team advocating for and supporting individuals in recovery. Through this role, I can shape policies and initiatives prioritizing access to resources, reducing stigma, and promoting holistic well-being. As a committee member for the merger between the Metropolitan Homelessness Commission and the COC Governance Board, I actively shape the future of homelessness services in our region. This collaborative effort has allowed me to contribute my insights and perspectives, ensuring that the voices of those affected are heard and respected.

Serving on the Licensure Board for the TN Department of Mental Health and Substance Abuse Services (TDMHSAS) has been a fulfilling experience. I actively engage in discussions and decisions that impact the quality and accessibility of mental health and substance abuse services throughout our state, striving to create an environment that fosters recovery and support for all.

Being a part of the Consumer Advisory Board planning committee for the Department of Metro Homelessness Commission has given me a platform to amplify the voices of individuals with lived experience. Through this committee, we develop strategies and policies that promote dignity, empowerment, and long-term solutions to homelessness.

In my involvement with the (TADDAS) Recovery Support and Criminal Justice Committee, I advocate for programs and initiatives that facilitate the successful reintegration of individuals involved with the criminal justice system. By championing their recovery and providing support, we break the cycle of recidivism and create opportunities for a brighter future.

Lastly, serving on the Certified Peer Recovery Specialist (CPRS) Committee has allowed me to contribute to the professional development and standards within the field of peer recovery support. By working together, we ensure that individuals providing these invaluable services receive the necessary training and support to make a meaningful difference in the lives of those they serve.

Before I took on these roles, I was a member of the (TADDAS) Recovery Support and Criminal Justice Committee. I actively contributed my insights and expertise to advocate for programs and initiatives that facilitated the successful reintegration of individuals involved with the criminal justice system. Together, we worked tirelessly to break the cycle of recidivism, offering support and hope for a brighter future.

One of my significant contributions was serving on the steering committee for the certified peer recovery specialist manual. In this role, I played an instrumental part in developing guidelines and standards for peer recovery specialists, ensuring they received the necessary training and support to make a meaningful difference in the lives of those they served. It was an honor to contribute to the professional development and growth of this vital role within the field of recovery support.

I also had the privilege of serving on the United Way Ryan White Review committee, where I actively reviewed and allocated resources to support individuals affected by HIV/AIDS. This experience allowed me to witness firsthand the transformative power of community support and collaboration in improving the lives of those impacted by this challenging condition.

Through my involvement with the National Alliance Recovery Residents Committee (NARR), I joined forces with like-minded individuals to advocate for the rights and well-being of individuals in recovery housing. Our efforts focused on ensuring safe and supportive environments for those on their journey to sobriety, fostering a sense of community and empowerment.

As a SAMHSA (Substance Abuse and Mental Health Services Administration) Regional Recovery Panel member, I worked closely with underserved populations. Together, we addressed their unique challenges and barriers in accessing essential mental health and substance abuse services. This experience deepened my understanding of the importance of equitable and inclusive care for all individuals, regardless of their background or circumstances.

Beyond committee work, I actively engaged in Narcotics Anonymous (NA) as a trusted servant. As a trusted servant,

I served as a General Service Representative (GSR), representing the needs and perspectives of the local NA community and contributing to the ongoing growth and development of the fellowship. I also had the honor of serving as the Program Chair for the Unity Convention of Narcotics Anonymous, overseeing the planning and execution of this transformative event that brought together individuals in recovery from all walks of life.

It's a blessing to do what I love and help those in need. But sometimes, when I look at all my work, I am hit with an intense whiplash because I clearly remember how difficult it was for me to work under active addiction.

During my journey, I had various jobs in addiction, but unfortunately, they did not last long. At one point, before things got terrible, I worked in the cafeteria at St. Thomas Hospital. It was a good job, but my addictive behaviors outweighed my ability to perform effectively. I stayed in that job for about a year before drugs took over my life. During that time, I became pregnant with my second child in 1988, and she was born in October 1989. I used drugs instead of returning in time to sign the necessary paperwork for my daughter's heart surgery. The doctors threatened to call Child Protective Services, but instead, they called my mom, who stepped in and signed the papers. I recall my mom saying that if I didn't want my baby, I should sign her over to her, but she made it clear that my daughter deserved better and that I needed to get my life together.

After that incident, I attempted to improve my situation. While working at St. Thomas Hospital, I was caring for my daughter when my friend Vicki Nunn reached out to me. She encouraged me to speak to our manager and explain that I needed help and that my insurance could provide assistance. I followed her advice and spoke to my supervisor, which led to them helping me find a treatment program at the old Baptist Hospital. I stayed in the program for 30 days, and afterward, my mom would bring my kids to visit me. However, after getting out, I attended support meetings for only about two months before falling back into my old habits. I entered into a toxic relationship, and when things went sour, I resorted to my familiar pattern of numbing the pain, escaping reality, and neglecting responsibility through drug use.

I am forever grateful for Vicki, who never judged me and always tried to distract me from using drugs. She would invite me to go to clubs or shop at the mall. While her sisters were involved in theft, she never participated. I, however, tried it once and got caught during my second attempt at stealing clothes at Rivergate Mall. It was an inside job, where we knew which employees were working during our shift, and we would place shopping bags under the clothes, allowing them to fall inside.

The trick was to leave with a group of shoppers when the alarm went off because there were so many people that the employees would often overlook it. My first attempt was successful, but the second time, I got caught, and I was sent to jail and placed on probation. That experience made me realize that stealing was not who I was. Interestingly, I had over **six hundred dollars** in my pocket on the day I was stealing. There was another job I had as a flag lady on Harding Place. I remember going to work heavily intoxicated on drugs. I almost caused a few accidents while trying to control traffic. Some drivers cursed me out and made offensive gestures towards me. On one occasion, I went to work in the winter and caught what I thought was a sore throat. It was strep throat, and I ended up in the hospital. The infection was severe, and I had to be placed in the ICU while they treated it in my throat and lungs. My mom was battling cancer at that time and was also caring for my two daughters. During my ICU stay, Vicki was the only person who visited me within the allotted hours.

After recovering from the ICU and returning home, I knew I couldn't return to that job due to the shame and guilt of my actions. I decided to try working at a warehouse, which only lasted a few weeks. My primary motivation was to receive that first paycheck to fuel my addiction further. This is where active addiction took complete control of my life, and I was caught in a cycle of incarceration, going in and out of jail multiple times. In my last arrest, I was involved in selling cocaine as a means of income, but my only purpose was to purchase more drugs and avoid taking responsibility for the life I believed was the key to wealth.

It's astonishing how we can perceive something seemingly simple but dangerous and still believe we are exempt from the risks.

Looking back on all aspects of my life, it's strange to see that nowadays, one of my deepest interests lies in advocating for affordable housing and recognizing the vital importance of safe and secure homes for individuals and families. By shedding light on this critical issue, I strive to contribute to positive change and create a world where everyone can access affordable and dignified housing.

Another significant area of focus for me is homelessness. Witnessing the struggles faced by those experiencing homelessness has fueled my determination to make a difference. I believe in the power of compassion, outreach, and community collaboration to bring about sustainable solutions and support individuals on their journey toward stable and fulfilling lives.

Recovery holds a special place in my heart, and I am passionate about sharing the message of hope and healing with individuals worldwide. Having experienced the transformative power of recovery, I am dedicated to supporting others in their journey toward sobriety, offering guidance, and inspiring them to embrace a life of freedom and purpose.

While actively pursuing my advocacy work, I also recognize the importance of balance and self-care. One of the ways I find solace and rejuvenation is by vacationing at the beach. There's something magical about the soothing sound of waves, the warmth of the sun on my skin, and the ocean's vastness that allows me to reconnect with myself and find tranquility amidst the chaos of life.

Above all, spending time with my family is the cornerstone of my joy and fulfillment. I am blessed with four children, each a source of inspiration and a reminder of the beautiful journey of parenthood. Watching them grow and thrive fills my heart with immeasurable pride and joy.

After the birth of my first child, Kenishea, I never envisioned myself building a large family – it simply wasn't my aspiration. But my path took a different turn due to addiction and my heedless choices. These choices led to a heartbreaking sequence of events – a miscarriage before my second child and two more before my third and final child.

In the aftermath, as the dust settled and I resumed parenting all three of my children, a profound sense of gratitude mingled with an overwhelming fear within me. This fear wasn't merely a passing emotion; it stemmed from my uncertainty about whether I could be a good parent. The years of abandonment and neglect I had subjected my children to cast doubt upon my ability to nurture them.

During this period of uncertainty, a lifeline emerged in the form of therapy. Through these therapeutic sessions, I embarked on a journey to mend and rebuild the fractured relationship with my kids. Each session became a steppingstone toward redemption, a chance to confront the consequences of my past actions. Within these therapeutic moments, I learned the importance of allowing my children to voice their feelings about my absence during my struggles with addiction and the burdens they had shouldered in my absence. Though not a quick fix, this process was an essential step in our collective healing as a family unit.

Admittedly, there were instances when I felt that my children would be better off under someone else's care. But it was my therapist, Ali Marlow, who offered a fresh perspective. She helped me recognize that the pain and effort were all worthwhile investments in their future.

This revelation and my commitment to change led me on a transformative path. Following my release, I engaged in an intensive two-year-long outpatient program involving individual and family therapy sessions. Looking back, I can firmly attest that this was the turning point in my life.

I stand with them as a testament to mothers who carry the burden of shame and embarrassment for not living up to their parental roles due to addiction. The clutches of addiction can induce a torturous state where promises are broken, intentions are overshadowed, and priorities get skewed. The promises I made to my children during my darkest hours were sincere, but the grip of addiction rendered them hollow. This disease, it seemed, had the power to wrest away my capacity to prioritize my children's well-being.

And this reminds me of another significant loss. Apart from working on Mending Hearts, Charlotte and I also embraced the role of parents to a blended family of four children. This journey was difficult, especially considering the challenges of raising biracial children in a world that sometimes struggled with acceptance. But together, we faced the nation, standing strong in our commitment. Our victory wasn't just in the legal battle for custody against her family in a small town; it was in raising these four children with love, resilience, and a shared bond that transcended even the end of our romantic relationship.

Despite our subsequent divorce, the love and connection between all four children remain unshaken. Their sibling relationship endures, a testament to the enduring strength of our blended family. Reflecting on the past, I'm convinced that we triumphed in our commitment to nurturing and supporting these children, each cherished as a relative.

Presently, my children and I have emerged stronger from our experiences. While not exempt from any family's challenges, we have established a healthier framework. Dysfunction no longer resembles the patterns I grew up with; we have created a space for open communication and genuine understanding.

Contrary to my upbringing, my children excel at addressing disagreements, even if it means stepping back before finding common ground. Unlike in the past, where differences were swept under the rug, my children have embraced the essential art of dialogue and resolution. I must credit my late mother for instilling this value in me during my formative years.

In the present landscape, I view my children not solely as my kids but as pillars of unwavering support. Whether confronted by a harrowing crisis or the mundanities of daily life, we stand united. The foundation we've built is trust and availability for one another. Though they lead their independent lives now, we still carve out moments to come together. I can now attend doctor appointments, celebrations, and pivotal decisions that shape their lives.

My children have generously allowed me to step into the role they longed for, and even on days when I'm not at my best, I possess the capacity to be a nurturing and compassionate mother.

And now, as a grandparent to four precious grandchildren, I am fortunate to experience the purest form of love and witness the wonders of life through their innocent eyes.

The journey was bone-crushing, yet the flight to freedom was being restored to all the limitless possibilities of life while being a member of society and living as others do. With the support of family, friends, and support networks, I'm grateful that I am alive.

Printed in the USA
CPSIA information can be obtained
at www.ICGtesting.com
LVHW091254100923
757642LV00001B/1